California Dreamin'

A 19-Year Old Indian Sikh's Memoir:

Journey to California, Romance, Trials &Tribulations

1953 Oldsmobile 98

The car I bought for my trip from Indiana to California.

(This was taken from a brochure. This is not my original car.)

California Dreamin'

A 19-Year Old Indian Sikh's Memoir:
Journey to California, Romance, Trials &Tribulations

_____

_____

Rajinder S. Khokhar

Kavita's picture on the back cover is a composite drawn from memory.

SP (1019)

Publisher

Rajinder S. Khokhar

Dedication

To my grandfather Bhai Budh Singh.

Also to Mom & Dad.

Acknowledgment

Deep thanks to my partner, Jacqueline Chohan, for her invaluable assistance. Her comments and encouragement made this book possible. She spent countless hours reading through it multiple times correcting my typos and other problems.

Note: The book contains explicit language and scenes.

Preface

This book is about my journey to America and my first two years in this country. It is based on journals about my life experiences here and letters I exchanged with Daddy. It is quite fortuitous I came across this treasure as I retired—just when I had time to go through them and put it together in book form.

The correspondence with Daddy and the journals were in English. I would like to point out English was not my first language. Actually it's my third language behind Punjabi and Hindi.

Daddy's early education in the English language was rudimentary. He was born to an illiterate farmer in northern India. In the village schools there was no English taught. After graduating high school he moved to Delhi and started reading English newspapers diligently. Mostly his English was self-taught. Later he joined the Indian Army, and we had to move every couple of years. The village mentioned above is our ancestral home and Daddy's birthplace.

I arrived in America in the early sixties, and one of the first things I purchased was a typewriter. That enabled me to write long, detailed letters to Daddy. I saved his letters and copies of the letters I wrote to him. I also kept journals about my activities and my shipboard romance with a beautiful young Indian woman. We noticed each other as we were getting aboard in Bombay. I had never seen a young Indian woman as tall as her. On the other hand she had not seen a young Indian man as tall as me. We had a wonderful two-week romance, but had to part in Genoa, Italy because she had a different itinerary. She was planning to visit me in Indiana, but we were crushed because they had to rush back because her grandmother in India had a heart attack.

A year later she came to visit me with her mother, and we had a wonderful two weeks together. Parting was very difficult, and we were heartbroken. I wondered if I would see her again. We kept in touch by letters, and it showed the difficulty of long-distance romances.

California Dreamin' details this nineteen-year-old's journey to America and trying to get a toehold in this country. It narrates my trials and tribulations. I wrote all about this in my letters home and also in my journals. Somehow I managed to keep my head above water and continue on. Here I was, a young man with no family support except for a lifeline with Daddy who sat twelve time zones away. He had no idea what I was really up against. All he could do was help keep me levelheaded while I was going ballistic. He was completely blind to the actual circumstances in America until I finally wrote him a very long letter about the difficulties I was facing. The letters we exchanged are included in the Appendix.

I was a very starry-eyed new arrival in America, and everything was new and fascinating. The first six months of my stay here were a dream, as I breezed through college in Indiana. I ran into an old classmate from the boarding school in India, and we had good adventures together. Mrs. Boriak, the wife of one of the professors took special interest in us foreign students and threw us a great dinner party. Later she learned I was leaving for California, and she had good advice about driving through the Rockies.

Then I was off to California for summer jobs. It was a very different story as I moved out of the college environment into the real world. I had the naïveté of a nineteen-year-old and that also showed. The hardest part was discrimination I faced in the California's Central Valley. Trying to find a job in the Fresno area was extremely tough for a turbaned Sikh, and I was turned down at more than a dozen places. Finally I got a job at a packinghouse through the sympathy of Nikos, a Greek foreman who knew my plight because he had been a foreign student himself, and I worked very hard not to let him down. Equally challenging was trying to find an apartment. All this was recorded in my journal and the letters I wrote to Daddy. Some of the observations and experiences were quite harsh, which came through in my letters. This march through history has many emotions swirling about in my mind.

I would like to emphasize what communication was like during early sixties. The fastest way was by telegraph, which was expensive because they charged by the word. After that was the telephone, which presupposed all parties having telephones, and my family did not have one. Letters were the main medium of communications overseas.

It is a miracle I found these letters and journals. They survived the move from Indiana to California and multiple moves in this state. They even survived a fire in 2007.

Introduction

Sometimes we need to look backward in order to move forward. My friend, Rajinder discovered a goldmine of letters he had exchanged with his Daddy decades earlier. Another goldmine was journal he had kept at the same time.

Catching a glimpse of who he was at age nineteen has been a profound experience for me. His parents had laid a solid foundation upon which Rajinder grew from a teen to a man after his arrival in America. Of course the senior Rajinder is very different from the nineteen-year-old youngster, yet the essence of who he was then is an integral part of who he is now.

As his story unfolded before me, what touched me deeply was the love between father and son. Every son dreams his father would respect his decisions and have tremendous faith and confidence in his choices and abilities. Every father dreams his son would grow into a man with a strong strength of character in order to be successful and happy. This father and son have accomplished this dream.

I'm amazed how emotionally mature Rajinder was at twenty. Many men don't reach his level of maturity until the age of forty or later, and some never do. I'm awed by his insights, how he has perceived his life experiences and how he handled life challenges. An example is his trip from Indiana to California. He kept his cool when a front tire blew at 85 mph and prevented a major catastrophe or loss of life.

I'm impressed by his emotional maturity at this point in his life, by his ability to reason and free associate. He has important insights on how to handle situations tactfully and diplomatically. In other words, he is able to walk in another's moccasins.

I am amazed by Rajinder's coping ability regarding a tall Indian woman he loved dearly and who appeared to be his soul mate. How does one carry on when one's heart desperately longs for the woman of his dreams? Carry on he did, for his future depended on his ability to move forward with his life.

Allow this nineteen-year-old to touch your heart, share his wisdom and his beautiful spirit with you. You will learn a lot about how to handle life.

Jacqueline Chohan

Friend

A Message in a Bottle
From Me in Early Sixties

California Dreamin' is my first of a trilogy—followed
by *Kavita, My Beloved* and *Kavita II*

Chapter 1

Off to America

My daddy and I were chilled to the bone by the icy December wind as we stood on the pier in Bombay. (Now known as Mumbai.) I was waiting to board the ship for the Genoa, Italy leg of my journey to America for higher studies. There was also the angst of leaving the security of home and family behind, but for this nineteen-year-old the sense of adventure far out-weighed all other emotional challenges. I was the only passenger who had just one person seeing me off. Everyone else had multitudes of well-wishers, and the side of the ship was awash with streamers. I had a difficult time saying good-bye to Daddy, and I was depressed. There was also the sense of excitement and anticipation of the new experiences and adventures to come.

We were boarding the ship, and my eyes were drawn to a tall young Indian woman on the other side of the gangplank. She was beautiful, fair-skinned with long flowing black hair and had an athletic build. I am six feet tall, and she was only a couple inches shorter than me. I had never seen that tall an Indian woman before. She was looking over the passengers, which was quite unusual for an Indian woman. She paused when our eyes met, and I thought I saw a faint smile. I was mesmerized by her and bumped into the man in front of me. I apologized and bent over to help retrieve the items he had dropped. The tall woman was gone when I stood up. Oh well, I chalked it up to my overactive imagination, but that look she gave me was definitely on my mind. I went up to the main deck to watch Daddy on the dock. I can still picture him standing off to one side, and I kept my eyes on him until he was no longer visible. He had not moved an inch. I wished Mom had been there to see me off, but we had said good-bye in Delhi because she was unable to make the journey to Bombay.

I got acquainted with other young Indians who were also traveling abroad for studies. Some were going to Germany, others to England and a few to America. Later we went to our cabins, and the steward came by to give us a rundown of the ship's routines as we unpacked.

Later I went in the direction the tall woman would have gone from her side of the gangplank. I came to a set of doors with a sign, First Class Passengers Only, which threw a bucket of ice-cold water in my face. Oh well, seemed like the connection ended even before it began. My walk back to my cabin was long and slow.

The ship was Italian and so was food, which we knew nothing about. The server was helpful and had us try different dishes. I looked for the tall Indian woman in the dining room, but did not see her. I finished early and stood by the exit, but there was no sign of her, and I was disappointed.

Next day we arrived in Karachi, Pakistan. Some of us youngsters got off the ship and went wandering around to see what we could find. There was a tourist information shack nearby, and we thought it was a good place to start. Turned out it was an official site, and they assigned one of the employees, Hanif to show us around. We toured the city, went to a lake, and enjoyed talking to the young man. In the evening we decided to buy him dinner, and he took us to a nice restaurant. The place seemed quite full, and the owner said he just didn't have room for that large a party. He saw me with my turban and beard and realized we were passengers from the ship. He scurried around, put tables together and served us a wonderful non-Italian meal.

We took a bus back to the port, and one of the local passengers recognized my being from Punjab, India. He said he was very unhappy about the partitioning of the country and asked me to convey his best wishes to others in the state of Punjab. I knew he was a resident of Punjab, Pakistan because he spoke perfect Punjabi. Punjab had been cut into two during the partition, and he was genuinely unhappy about losing his Sikh and Hindu friends. With that he left, and I was unable to talk to him further. I had no memory of anything he was talking about because I was only five at the time, but I was deeply touched by his comments. That was a very traumatic time for India because everything was turned upside down, and he was genuinely unhappy with the breakup of the country. We arrived back at the port and thanked Hanif for the wonderful day we had touring Karachi. He thanked us for dinner and wished us a wonderful journey. Also I mailed postcards to Mom and Daddy.

The following day all the young Indian passengers were getting acquainted while enjoying the sunshine on the main deck. We were playing shuffleboard and having a jolly good time trying to get the hang of the game. None of us could get anything right because we hadn't played the game before.

Opening of the elevator doors drew my attention, and there was just one person stepped out—the tall Indian woman. She smiled and waved as she noticed me, and I smiled and waved back. Her long black hair was blowing in the gentle breeze, and the scarf around her neck seemed to be waving me hello. She was wearing flat-heeled sandals for obvious reason. I thought she looked wonderful in the baby blue sari when I first saw her on the gang plank, but it paled in comparison with the hip hugging blue Western dress she had on, and I was mesmerized. That also threw me into a bit of panic because in comparison I seemed to be dressed as a beggar. Fortunately our eyes had locked, and I didn't think she noticed what I was wearing.

My friends were intrigued and couldn't believe how tall she was. After a while she walked to the railing with a backward glance. I got a lot of kidding from my friends as they pushed me in her direction. I didn't need any pushing or prodding because I wanted to run over, introduce myself and give her a big hug before she disappeared again. Unfortunately, my feet were acting as if my shoes were glued to the deck. I covered that up by telling them they were reading too much into this, and there was no way anyone like her would be interested in me. I had a feeling she was aware of what was going on and was enjoying the show. Finally she left, but the ribbing from my friends continued.

I went below to my cabin because I was not happy about my friends' routines. It would have been a lot different if they had discretely backed off and let us be. Later I went for a walk on the main deck to keep away from them. I was surprised to see the tall Indian woman walking in front of me as I rounded a corner. I was fascinated and a bit apprehensive because she would be turning around at the end of the walkway and wondered what I would say to her when we came face-to-face. I watched her while keeping the same distance between us. She noticed me when she turned around, and her whole face lit up with a radiant smile likes of which I had never seen before. It was a smile that said, 'About time you showed up! Where have you been?' She stopped in front of me and asked, "Are you following me?" She turned around and walked with me. I was a bit flustered and had trouble moving my legs. I smiled sheepishly and tried to act as if it was just another walk, but failed miserably in my effort to appear suave and sophisticated. My self-confidence fell onto the deck and lay there like a lump of goo. It took all my will power to put one foot in front of the other, and my sheepish smile was replaced by a silly grin. I wondered what she must have been thinking of my bumbling ways. All this seemed to last an eternity, but it was only a few steps. Quickly I regained my senses and replied, "Not really. You happened to be ahead of me on this walk. It could just as easily have been the other way around."

She took my hand and said, "That is true. Hello, my name is Kavita."

"Hello Kavita, my name is Rajinder. It's a pleasure to finally meet you."

"Hello Raajindiaer. It is very nice to meet you, too."

She had trouble pronouncing my name. She mangled it. I put my hand on top of hers and said, "It's Ra—jin—der."

"Okay, Rajinder it is."

She did better at pronouncing it. She held on to my hand as we walked, and said, "Why didn't you catch up with me and introduce yourself?"

"I wanted to, but my legs weren't responding."

"I find that hard to believe. No matter. Important part is we finally meet."

"Yes, and sorry about earlier. It was quite a challenge with everybody having fun at my expense. I hope you weren't too disappointed."

"Not really. I was amused, and I thought you handled it well. Your friends were relentless."

"You didn't see the rest of it. I got quite a ribbing." I looked at her and continued, "But it was worth it."

She smiled, "Thank you, I was hoping you'd say that."

"I'm glad you didn't give up because I was hoping to meet you. You had my full attention on the gangplank."

"Yes, I'm glad you noticed me because I sure noticed you."

"Of course I noticed you! There was the crowd of passengers and there were you. I have never seen an Indian woman as tall and beautiful as you. You really got my attention."

"I haven't seen a young Indian man as tall and handsome as you. Of course you got my attention! Okay, now we can start our own *Mutual Admiration Club.*"

We laughed, and it was lovely hearing her laugh. She was holding my hand tightly as if to keep me from getting away. I looked at her and then down to our hands. She got the message and loosened her grip and said, "Sorry, I wasn't aware I was hurting you."

"No big deal. I promise I won't run away!"

She blushed. "Have you traveled overseas before?"

"No, this is my first voyage out of the country."

She looked surprised. "I thought you had done this before because you seem very self-assured."

"Kind of you to say that. My guess is you have done this before."

She smiled and said, "Yes. This is my third voyage. I've been to England once and to America twice. So where are you headed?"

"I'm going to America for studies. Where are you headed?"

She seemed pleased, "America! We are going to the state of Virginia. Daddy also has business in Washington, D.C. We will be stopping in England to see Daddy's friends. Where in America are you going?"

"To the state of Indiana."

We didn't know where those states were. We walked in silence for a while, and I was feeling quite relaxed around her. In college there were no women in my Engineering classes, and I didn't even have a sister. In other words, I had no experience with women and was in uncharted territory. At the time there was no dating and very little mixing of the sexes in India.

Rather hesitatingly she asked, "What is your cabin number?"

"165."

I saw some of my friends walking ahead of us, and I said, "I'm not sure how we can keep away from them."

"Come with me."

We ducked into a hallway, and she led me on a convoluted path to the first class section. I asked, "How did you know about this side of the ship? Weren't you in first class on your last trip?"

"I went exploring because I didn't have much to do."

"So that is how you knew how to meander your way to the first class section. That sure came in handy!"

She said, "There is no way they can follow us in here."

"You sure they won't throw me out?"

"You are with me. Would you like a cup of tea?"

We sat down and she ordered tea. We talked about where we were from and minor generalities. She was from Madhya Pardesh, which is right in the midsection of India. I told her I was from Punjab, which is north of Delhi. She hadn't done much travelling in India, but had accompanied her parents overseas on her father's business trips. Too soon she had to get back before her parents missed her. I took her hand and pulled her to me for a cursory hug. She looked at me and smiled before walking away. That was the first time I didn't have to bend over to hug a woman.

The following morning I familiarized myself with the ship's amenities. There was shuffleboard, dart games, Italian lessons and American Western movies. I tried my hand at shuffleboard again and an older gentleman defeated me handily. After he left I kept trying shots to get a feel for the game. I thought about Kavita because I hadn't seen her on deck. There was not much I could do because I couldn't go to her side of the ship. After lunch we went to our cabins for a nap, and later we decided to take in the western movie. After dinner we went up to the main deck for a long walk. We were going back to our cabins, and I was lagging behind because I was lost in my thoughts. Out of the corner of my eye a movement caught my attention. It was Kavita signaling me from the shadows, and I pretended to tie my shoelaces. The guys yelled at me to hurry up or they'd leave me behind. She came over to pull me to my feet as they went around a corner.

"What quick thinking—tying your shoelaces."

"I had to think fast. That was the only thing that came to mind."

"I just had to see you. I couldn't find you earlier."

"I was busy with my friends. We took in a movie, played shuffleboard for some time and went for a walk. I would have rather been with you."

"I'm sorry I didn't come looking for you at that time."

We took a walk on the main deck. She put her arm around me and I did likewise. Not much was said, and we just enjoyed being with each other. She saw me eyeing a bench and said, "There's a lounge nearby, and it'll be warmer in there."

We walked in there, and it turned out to be a small movie theater. Kavita was surprised and whispered, "I'm sorry. On my last trip it was a lounge."

We sat down on a back couch to watch the movie, but our attention was on each other. There was one other person watching the movie, and she left shortly after we arrived. We embraced and had our cheeks against each other. That was very nice, and she ran her hand up and down my back. I did likewise and ran my fingers through her hair. She smiled at me and said she liked that. A couple walked in and we pulled apart to watch the movie for a while. Too soon Kavita said it was late, and she had to get back. We arrived at the entrance to her section, and she put her arms around me for a bear hug. I watched her as she turned and walked away. It was a very sensual hug, and I was tingling all over.

I slowly walked back to my cabin, and my friends were waiting for me on my bunk. I tried to shoo them away, but they wanted to know what kept me. I told them Kavita attracted my attention, and that was why I had the sudden urge to tie my shoelaces. They couldn't believe they fell for such a stupid ruse. One of them had gone back to check, but found no sign of me. They decided to wait on my bunk so they could grill me. I said there was not much to tell. We had gone up to the deck for a walk. After that we went to the movie theater for a while, and I walked her to the first class section. They booed and were not happy they had stayed around for that little tidbit. I told them I was a good storyteller and could make something up, but they booed again and walked out.

Next morning we tried to get Indian radio station on our portable radio, but had no luck. I tried my hand at shuffleboard again and did a bit better. Seemed like most of those who played were experienced travelers and knew the game. Those who didn't know the game didn't bother trying.

Later I found a note from Kavita on my bunk.[1] I met her, and we went for a walk in the first class section where we would be safe from prying eyes of my friends. Kavita was wearing western clothes, which turned out to be a problem because her skirt was being blown around by

---

[1]   There were no phones in the cabins at the time.

the swirling wind. She was trying hard to keep it down, but to no avail. She was struggling to get to a protected corner, but a gust of wind lifted her skirt clear up her back exposing her naked behind. I was embarrassed, and had a bit of a smirk on my face.

She asked, "Alright, what did you see?"

I kept quiet and avoided her eyes, but the smirk on my face was still there.

"Okay, don't tell me. Just look at what you saw."

I couldn't help but look at her behind. She snickered and gave me a hug as if I was forgiven. She was blushing from the moment her skirt went flying.

"There's no way I could have avoided seeing a naked behind that popped up in front of me. You can poke my eyes out if you want."

"No way would I do that! I'll go change, but speak now if you don't want me to change."

"Why wouldn't I want you to change?"

She smiled, "You might be hoping to see more."

"Kavita, seeing more is every man's fantasy, but now isn't the time or place. Incidentally, very lovely!"

"Thank you. I'll be right back."

Luckily there was no one else around at the time. I played shuffleboard to occupy myself, and a gentleman asked if we could play a game or two. I told him I was a rank beginner and wouldn't be offering much competition. Turned out he was also a beginner, and neither of us could get anything right, but we had a jolly good time laughing at each other's shots. A steward asked if there was anything we wanted. He ordered a beer and asked if I wanted one too. I declined, but he ordered one for me anyway, and we chatted. He was a British businessman returning to London and was taking a flight out of Rome. I told him I was on my way to America for higher studies. Kavita got back, and I introduced him. She saw the beer in front of me and asked why I wasn't drinking it. I took a couple of sips and offered it to her. She took a couple of sips and then we begged our leave. She had changed to another skirt, which was not affected by the swirling wind. She twirled in front of me and said, "Too bad this skirt won't fly up for you! I hope you aren't disappointed."

"Kavita, with you I'm never disappointed."

"This ship stops in Genoa. How are you getting to America from there?"

"I'll take a train to Calais, France and then the ferry across the English Channel to Dover. From there I take the train to London and then on to America by air."

She looked at me incredulously and was fascinated I was undertaking this momentous journey alone.

She asked, "So how old are you?"

"I am nineteen."

She was taken aback. "I can't believe you are only nineteen. I thought you were older."

"At times I wish I was older. Mostly I think I'm just about the right age. How old are you, if you don't mind my asking?"

She looked at me and thought for a moment. She finally said, "I'm twenty-two. I thought you were older than me."

"Am I too young for you?"

"Not at all. Although I figured your age to be at least twenty-four."

I smiled at her sheepishly and said, "I was just pulling your leg. I am twenty-seven."

"There is one way to settle this. Let me see your passport."

"You got me. I really am nineteen."

She smiled, "I don't want to be accused of robbing the cradle. It's all right with me if you want to be twenty-seven, but I prefer you to be nineteen."

It was my turn to be cute, "I know, so you can mother me, and tell me what to do and what not to do."

She gave me a stern look. "I don't want to hear that again, or I'll have to call you baby."

I smiled broadly. It was a, 'I know something you don't' smile. "What are you smiling about? I didn't say anything funny."

"In a way you did. I've heard in America baby is a very endearing word. For example, if you really liked me you would be apt to call me baby."

She was not happy with that comment. "And what do they call real babies?"

"I don't know all the details about America. I do know about being called baby because that is what I've seen in movies. I'd love it if you called me baby, but only if you meant it, that is."

"I'll keep that in mind. What will you be studying?"

"Electronics. Are you going to college or a university?"

"I have a Bachelor of Arts degree. I am thinking of going for a Master's degree when I get back. Do you have a degree?"

"I have a B. S. degree from Punjab University."

She was quite surprised, "I just got my B.A. last year. How did you get a B.S. at your age?"

"By working hard. Actually very, very hard!"

"You are going to be difficult, aren't you? Now tell me how it is you got a B.S. degree by nineteen? How old were you when you graduated from high school?"

"I was sixteen."

"You graduated from high school at sixteen? And it took you only three years to get your degree? How is that possible?"

"I have Senior Cambridge diploma from Cambridge University in England. That put me one year ahead of other high school graduates, which allowed me to get my degree in three years. Would you like to see my diploma?"

"I have never heard of a Senior Cambridge diploma. How did you know about it?"

"I didn't. Daddy handled all that, and I just followed orders. So here I am."

Kavita finished her tea. "I have to get back. It was a real pleasure seeing you again. May I see you tomorrow?"

"Of course, I'd like that, and I enjoyed seeing you, too."

She smiled back at me. "I'll send you a note."

She looked into my eyes as we hugged. I had never had a long conversation with a girl. I didn't even have a sister, and that was quite a handicap for me. I attended an all-boys boarding school for five years. Also there were very few women in college at the time. Kavita made me feel as if we had known each other for a long time.

I felt pretty good as I headed up to the main deck, and my friends were wondering what I had been up to. I told them about the note and meeting with Kavita. Of course they wanted all the details, and I provided some tidbits. They wanted to know when I was going to see her again, and I told them I didn't know because she might not want to have anything to do with me considering my age. They kidded me a lot, and I took it gracefully because I knew the reason for that was they wished it had happened to them.

Kavita and I got together daily and stayed mostly in first class section where we watched movies, played shuffleboard and other games. She arranged to have our pictures taken by the ship's photographer. She had her meals with her parents, and I had my meals with my friends. They kidded me about ignoring them, and I said I was sitting there for them to chastise me all they wanted. They were quite bugged because they couldn't wipe that silly grin off my face. They just wanted to know something about my time with her, and they listened intently although they knew I was not going into any detail. Their ribbing was well intentioned because dating was extremely uncommon in India. It was very unusual what was going on between Kavita and me because at the time all marriages in India were arranged.

This involvement with Kavita had me thinking about our relationship. Our eyes met when we were boarding the ship, and I thought I saw a hint of a smile. Could it be that smile was really there and was not just my overactive imagination? I was with my friends the first time I saw her on deck. She smiled and waved at me, and I did likewise. My friends were pushing me in her direction, and she seemed amused. Later we met on deck while she was taking a walk, which had me wondering what she was doing on my side of the ship because there was a perfectly good area for walks in the first class section. She accused me of following her, but turned around and walked with me. We continued on and turned around just as she had done moments earlier. I hadn't thought anything about it at the time. 'So she had come looking for me,' was my thought.

Kavita and I talked about boarding the ship. She told me, "I was looking over the crowd before boarding the ship. I noticed you with your father, and I was wondering which one of you was coming aboard. I was hoping it would be you."

I was surprised, "Oh really? You had your eyes on me even before I got aboard?"

"Yes, I did."

"So you were watching me when we were on the dock? That explains it."

"That explains what?"

I said, "I had an eerie feeling as if I was being watched. I looked around, but didn't see anyone looking at me. I dismissed it as my imagination."

"Yes, I remember your looking around, and I figured you were expecting someone else to join you. Little did I know it was me you were looking for! Anyway, actually I had you on my mind a lot earlier."

"How can that be? There's no way you could have known me."

"That is true. I haven't told this to anyone, and it will sound quite far-fetched. I've been seeing a mysterious man in my dreams. I only saw his silhouette—tall, with full beard and a turban, but his face eluded me, and I often wondered if I would ever meet him. On the pier I was looking around to see if I could spot the man of my dreams."

"Well, did you?"

"Yes, I did."

The look she gave me was typical, 'Don't you understand? It seems to me I will have to lay it out for you.'

She said, "Luckily I'm able to see above the heads of almost everyone. My eyes were drawn to you standing there with your daddy. I was mesmerized—is that him, the man in my dreams?"

That hit me like a ton of bricks. I'd been called a lot of things, but never 'man in my dreams.' I stood there like a dummy, not knowing what to say. I decided 'If you don't know what to say—keep your mouth shut' was my best option. I was almost moved to tears along with the awkward feeling of, 'Me? Man of her dreams?' And I wondered what it meant to be the man in her dreams. I'd never dated a girl, let alone been a man in anyone's dreams. This was absolutely bizarre. She continued, "I lost track of you when we started boarding, and I was looking around to see if you were coming aboard. I smiled and waved hello when our eyes met, but I was disappointed when you looked down and disappeared from view."

"I bumped into the gentleman ahead of me because I was looking at you and not watching my step. I apologized and bent over to help pick up the hand luggage he had dropped. You were gone when I looked for you."

"That explains it. I thought you were avoiding me, and I wasn't sure what you'd think when I came looking for you."

"Kavita, I missed the part of your smiling at me and waving. I just saw the beginning of your smile. I wish I'd seen your smile because I might have bounded over and given you a big hug."

"Oh yes. That would have gone over wonderfully with my parents. My daddy would have had you arrested." She looked at me from head to toe and added, "I don't think he would have tried to beat you up."

"Just as well I didn't see that smile because it became extra special when I did."

I had thought it was rather strange she was looking over the passengers. Evidently she was checking to see if I was coming aboard.

The ship arrived at Aden, a free port at the southern tip of the Saudi Arabian Peninsula. I was hoping to go ashore with Kavita, but she went with her parents. I enjoyed walking the shopping district and bought a watch that was cheaper than similar ones in India. We were all poor students and didn't have much money to spend. One of my fellow travelers had a relative living there, and he took us on a tour of the city. Kavita was waiting for me on the main deck when I got back. We walked to the first class section and sat down for a cup of tea. We talked about her shopping adventure in Aden, and I asked her what she had bought. She stood up and twirled around. I was confused and looked at her questioningly.

She said, "I bought this dress. Do you like it?"

"Yes. It looks wonderful on you."

She seemed to be miffed as we were walking to the first class section. She said, "I'm sorry about being a little short with you earlier. I was upset you didn't notice my new dress …"

"Kavita, how could I have known? I don't know your wardrobe. I know you are always wearing something different and wonderful."

"Thank you. I'm sorry for my behavior because I realize you couldn't have known this was a new dress. Forgive me?"

"There is nothing to forgive. From here on I will compliment you for wearing a new dress every time I see you in something I haven't seen before. Would that be satisfactory?"

"Oh you! Serves me right for being so touchy. So how was your trip ashore?"

"We went exploring, and I bought a watch. One of the guys has a relative living there, and he took us on a tour. Nothing quite as exciting as buying myself a new dress!"

"Okay, I deserved that!"

She gave me a hug, and we went for a walk. We talked about our respective hopes and aspirations. She was not sure what she wanted to do after getting her master's degree because she had never really thought much about it. There were times I thought she was just amusing herself with me, but most of the time she was very affectionate and caring. She gave me pictures taken by the ship's photographer, and I was very happy to receive them including a framed photo of the two of us in a rather romantic pose.

She was jealous about my free-spirited journey across the globe by myself. She asked when I would be in London. I would be arriving on December twenty-second and leaving on the twenty-fifth. They would be arriving on December twenty-sixth. Normally one would say, 'Funny how this came about.' There was nothing funny about this. Somehow we had been brought together, and it looked like something was afoot to keep us apart. We were both saddened by this turn of events because none of it made sense. She couldn't change her itinerary and neither could I. She asked what I was going to do in London during my stay. I was apprehensive about telling her I was meeting my pen pal, Marina, but decided to go with the expression 'honesty is the best policy.' I said, "I will be meeting my long time German pen pal, Marina."

She looked at me suspiciously. "Hmm. A German pen pal, huh? When were you going to tell me about her? And how long have you known her?"

"Kavita, I'm sorry I didn't say anything. She slipped my mind completely because you had me so fascinated."

"Likely story!"

"Can I start from the beginning?"

"Please do! I'm dying to see how you are going to wiggle out of this!"

"This started out as a class project six years ago...."

She was very surprised. "Six years ago?"

"Yes. A bunch of us kids at my boarding school wrote letters to possible pen pals all over the world."

"So you wrote to Marina. How did you know her?"

"I didn't...."

"This is getting more and more bizarre. You didn't know her, but you wrote to her."

"Would you please let me explain?"

She nodded and I continued. "Our English teacher brought up the subject. Some of us students wrote letters and handed them to him. These were generic letters with no particular recipient in mind. He forwarded them to a clearing house where they had names and addresses of other kids from all over the world looking for pen pals." She was intrigued. I continued, "Some of us received replies to our letters from around the world."

Kavita was blown away. She asked, "So you got a reply from Marina?"

"Yes. Three months had gone by, and I had forgotten all about that letter. I was in Delhi after leaving the boarding school. One day Daddy came home from work and handed me a letter that had been forwarded from the boarding school. I looked at the return address—Germany. I was surprised and opened it with great anticipation. Marina introduced herself and said she was really looking forward to corresponding with me. With Daddy's help I composed a reply and sent it off to her. That started a wonderful friendship, and we have been corresponding since."

"And you never met her?"

"There was really no way for us to meet. Then my trip to America came up, and I told her I would be passing through London. We figured it was the perfect time for us to meet, and she said she would come to London. I want to assure you there is nothing romantic going on.

If there were then I would have run the other way when you came looking for me. It wouldn't have mattered whether I was the man of your dreams or not!"

"So you would have spurned me?"

"You could put it that way."

"You wouldn't have been concerned about breaking my heart?"

"Let's not get carried away because breaking someone's heart only comes after involvement. I wouldn't have noticed you on the gangplank and ignored you when you came up that elevator. On the other hand I would have been completely out of luck if you'd been involved with someone. You wouldn't have noticed me on the dock and would've ignored me on the gangplank. I couldn't have come looking for you in the first class section!"

She gave me a hug and said, "You do have a point! I really do understand. Lucky neither of us was involved with others!"

"There was a nasty incident involving one of the pen pal responses."

"Oh, ya? What happened?"

"One of my classmates got a reply from an Australian kid. He wrote, 'You damn blackie! How dare you write to me!'"

"Wow. An Australian kid? That is unbelievable. What did you guys do?"

"Nothing. The teacher was very upset and apologized to the whole class. We told him it was not his fault. He commented that he would send the response to the clearing house so that Australian kids' names were taken off their lists."

"Yes. Actually he deserved something a lot harsher."

We talked about her arrival in America, and I realized she would be arriving after my birthday. She noticed a change in my expression and wanted to know why. I tried to brush it off, but she wouldn't listen. Finally I admitted she would be arriving after my birthday. I was hoping she would make it special by being there, and we were both disappointed. We went for a walk, and I noticed she was wearing the skirt that had been blown around by the wind, but there was no danger of that because the surface of the sea was smooth as glass.

I commented, "Lucky we are not on a sailing ship. We would be going nowhere fast!"

She pulled herself to me for a hug. "That's true. Sure would have given us a whole lot more time together."

"Maybe not because the captain might have ordered me to man the oars!"

We went for a walk. I was concerned I might have upset her because she was a bit short with her answers. Also we bumped into each other as we came to a turn because she went one way and I went the other. I was following our normal walk we had been taking, and she had decided to go in a different direction. She apologized and said she should have warned me. We ended up in the area of the ship away from normal traffic. Kavita leaned over the railing, and I did likewise. I was going to say something, but she put her hand up to stop me, and put her finger to her lips. We looked at each other for a while, and I was unsure what to do next. She took care of that by putting her arms around my neck and pulling herself to me hard. This sudden movement pushed me against the bulkhead with her body pressing against me. I had to pull on her arms pretending to gasp for breath because her embrace was squeezing me tightly. She loosened her grip, but kept the body pressure up. I put my arms around her waist, and we were in this embrace for some time. I had never been held like this and it felt wonderful. I tingled all over, and she was shivering slightly.

Her tight embrace, her body fragrance and her breath on my neck were very arousing. I was embarrassed because I was poking at her, and I felt her breathing harder. She slowly moved her arms down in a bear hug and giggled as she looked at me. I couldn't push her back, and she looked at me with her mischievous smile while as she kept the pressure on. I was pretty much at her mercy because she had me pinned against the bulkhead. She was laughing and reveling at my discomfort.

"You remember what you saw the last time I wore this skirt?"

I was embarrassed by the question. "Yes."

She grabbed my hands and moved them to her behind. "You might as well get a feel of it."

I was doubly embarrassed and moved my hands up. She pushed them down and held them there. I could see she was quite flushed as she put her cheek against mine. That meant her breath was blowing in my ear, which made matters worse. I decided to reciprocate by blowing in her ear. She took a deep breath and froze for a few seconds. She said, "You are a rascal, aren't you? What are you trying to do by blowing in my ear?"

"What am I trying to do to you? You were blowing in my ear, and I was only reciprocating."

"I'm sorry. I didn't know I was doing that."

To emphasize that point she blew in my ear again. We had a few exchanges, and she leaned back to look at me. She was quite flushed, and I was very aroused. I turned her around so her back was toward the bulkhead. I pulled her skirt up in the back and fondled her naked butt. Her mouth fell open, as she was smiled broadly.

She said softly, "I didn't know blowing in your ear has this effect."

"Same here. I thought you knew what you were doing when you blew in my ear."

After a while she pulled back and looked at me. I was wondering if she was expecting me to kiss her. I sure wanted to, but kissing was not done in our culture. Besides, I didn't see her purse her lips because that is what I had seen in western movies. I had decided to let her take the lead because that was what she had done in every other facet of our relationship so far. I wondered if she was disappointed I didn't kiss her. I was certainly disappointed she didn't kiss me.[2]

She laughed and said, "Oh, that was wonderful."

I asked, "How did you find this place?"

Kavita gave me a mischievous look. "I was exploring. Oh, who am I kidding! I was looking for a place like this, and I'm glad I found it."

"So am I."

We went in for a cup of tea, and she reached for my hand under the table, which was obscured by the tablecloth. I looked at her, and she smiled as she put my hand on her thigh. She. I took her hand and put it on my thigh. I pushed my hand up her skirt and squeezed her thigh. She put her hand on top of mine and gave it a squeeze. Too soon it was time for her to leave. Reluctantly we got up, and she told me she would see

---

[2]   Regarding not kissing in India: you don't touch other people's food with hand or a utensil one has been eating with. Not kissing on the lip would be the logical extension of that custom. This is my take on this subject—not sure if this is the real reason.

me the following day. I was flying high as I went to the main deck. My friends rushed over and started peppering me with questions. I had a very smug look on my face and mostly ignored them. I was grateful they couldn't go to the first class section because they might have taken turns discreetly following us.

The following day I didn't see Kavita on the deck. Later I found a note on my bunk saying she would be sending a steward at seven for something special. I figured it was for dinner with her, and I was quite apprehensive because her parents would be there. At the appointed hour I was ready. I was dressed in my finest, although that was not saying very much. The steward led me to a private dining room, and what I saw stopped me dead in my tracks. Kavita was sitting on the couch, and the room was nicely decorated with runners and balloons. Behind her was a sign 'Happy Birthday, Rajinder.' I was having trouble taking it all in. She got up and grabbed me in a bear-hug. She asked, "Do you like it?"

"Kavita, this is unbelievable. I've never seen anything like it, and really feel honored! I don't know what to say except thank you very much."

The steward opened a bottle with a loud pop, poured two glasses and passed them to us. She said, "This is champagne. Hope you like it."

She clinked her glass against mine and said, "Happy birthday, Rajinder and many happy returns."

"Thank you, Kavita. This is absolutely delightful, and you really went all out."

The steward left and we sat down on the couch. We sipped the champagne as we looked into each other's eyes. She snuggled up to me, and I put my arm around her. I realized she had been busy and that was the reason I hadn't seen her on deck.

"I won't be in America for your birthday so I decided to bring it forward. I hope you don't mind."

"Of course I don't mind. What a question. You made this occasion very special, and I'm overwhelmed. Does this mean you didn't like me being nineteen?"

She said, "Yes, you got me there. Now you are twenty and no longer a teenager!"

"In other words I'm all grown up! Look out world, here I come!"

We laughed, and I looked at her admiringly. She wore a low cut blouse that seemed to be a size too small, and she was not wearing a bra. The top button was unfastened, and those were snap buttons. She was also wearing the skirt that had been blown around by the wind. She saw me noticing and had a very mischievous smile on her face. I opened my eyes about double the size, as I looked her up and down. "You look fantastic. All I can say is wow!"

She got up, took a bow and her breasts almost fell out of her blouse. I also got up and pulled her to me for a hug a little hard.

"Oh, you like to play rough, do you?"

She backed up and pulled me to her harder. We hugged and sat down. "I'm glad you like what I'm wearing. I wrapped myself in this shawl to get past Mom and Daddy."

She covered herself in the shawl hanging over the back of a chair, and with that on she looked quite demure. We sipped champagne and talked. She asked about my drinking habits, and I recounted my first experience with beer. I was at the officers' quarters in Kashmir with my daddy. He was the unit commander, and all of his junior officers were there. They poured me a glass of beer and wanted me to drink it. I looked at Daddy, and he gave me a slight nod. They harassed and cajoled me into drinking the beer. Daddy sat there and let those officers push me around. Kavita was amused. I asked if she had tried drinks before. She had very limited experience and had tasted champagne before. She enjoyed the tingly feeling she got from the bubbles. She said her mom had given her a strict curfew, and she had to be back by then.

There was a soft knock on the door, and the steward came in pushing a trolley. We sat down at the nicely decorated dining table, and I was flabbergasted as he removed the lids with a flourish. Here was a sumptuous Indian feast in front of us. She was happy to see my reaction and said she had the dinner specially prepared for us.

She wanted to know more about my past. "You talked about being in a boarding school. I can't imagine being away from Mom and Daddy."

"I understand, but I had no choice in the matter. Daddy decided that was best for me and dropped me off there rather unceremoniously."

"How did that happen?"

"At the time Daddy was a junior army officer, and he got the worst postings. He was away on duty at non-family stations, and I was attending the small one-room school in the village. The teacher retired, and there was no replacement available. A few of us kids were enrolled in the school in the next village. We would walk there in the morning and back in the afternoon."

"Wow, going to school in the next village? How far was that?"

"It might have been a couple of miles each way. Along the way there was an irrigation canal. It was hot, and on the way back we would take a dip to cool off."

"That must have been nice. Did you know how to swim?"

"No. None of us knew how to swim."

"Was there an adult accompanying you?"

"We were on our own. Finally Daddy found the boarding school."

"It must have been tough being away from your mom and daddy."

"Yes it was, but I had no choice in the matter."

"How old were you?"

"I was seven, and I was there for five years."

She could hardly believe what she was hearing. "I thought this solo trip you are taking is quite something, but I'm having trouble wrapping my head around what you just told me. Wait till my mother hears about this."

"How will your mother come to know about all this?"

"How do you suppose I managed to arrange this dinner?"

"I have no idea. Actually I don't want to know."

"She helpcd sct it up."

"Your mother knows about me?"

"No, she does not. She knows there is someone I'm interested in and she suggested a private dinner. With her help I made this your birthday dinncr by bringing it forward."

"You know she will have a thousand questions."

"I can handle Mom—don't worry about her."

"Kavita, that is easy for you to say. You are an only child, and parents don't take lightly to the likes of me getting too close to someone like you."

She gave me a very affectionate hug, "I told you not to worry."

"Right, I will be sleeping with one eye open all the way to Genoa."

"Ooh, I like the sound of that! Can I come by and check? What time did you say you go to sleep?"

"You mean half-asleep? You come to check and your daddy follows. You got me scared already, and I'm sorry I gave you my cabin number. I'll see if I can switch with one of my friends."

"Come on, you think they will help you? After the way you have been neglecting them they will be more than happy to help me."

"That's okay if they help you. I'll be fine so long as they don't help your daddy."

We laughed and hugged. I asked, "So how was it being an only child? Must have been a blast having mom and daddy all to yourself."

"Everyone says that, but it's nothing like that. Yes, I had Mom and Daddy to myself, but that also meant they concentrated on me, and there are no siblings to distract them. Not that I'm complaining, but sure would have been nice to have a sister."

"That's funny. That's what I've been thinking—sure would have been nice having a sister."

She laughed, "Yes, but you have a brother, which must have been nice."

"Part way true, but I had a brother sporadically. I was five when he was born, and at age seven I went to the boarding school for five years. Then we were together from age thirteen to nineteen. That was a challenge because he was just a baby when I left for the boarding school. He was eight when I came back home, and he was just a kid nipping at my heels."

"I can sympathize. From my point of view even a kid sister nipping at my heels would have been nice. I saw some of my friends with younger siblings. They did fight, but all in all they were happy to have them."

"I know. I have a lot of cousins, and most of them have five to seven brothers and sisters where you'd get lost in the shuffle. I really sympathized with the younger ones who were craving attention."

"I understand. I can't imagine having six or seven brothers and sisters, which is the other extreme. Let me put it this way. I'm happy to be the only child although I wouldn't have minded a little sister. Sure wouldn't have wanted an older sister. Some of my friends were in that situation, and it was as if they had two mothers!"

"I guess girls need to practice up! Sure glad I'm the elder. Being the younger would not have been any fun. I have seen elder brothers order their younger siblings around. At least I didn't do that to my brother."

"You were saving that part for me?"

"How can that be? Need I remind you that I'm younger than you?"

"Oh please! Don't remind me. On second thought, I like that. I'm the elder and you have to kowtow to me!"

"Yes Ma'am! Anything your heart desires. I'll have to talk to your mother about adopting a son and make sure he is older than you. Then you'll really find out how it is for me being the youngster!"

"Oh you! How impossible can you get? You know, I really enjoy our bantering. Anyway, you were asking about my being the only child. I love it and wouldn't have it any other way. They spoiled me rotten and granted me all my wishes. Compared to my friends I got away with murder! There is a rather large down side, though."

I asked, "What would that be? I can't imagine there being any downside."

"All their hopes, aspirations and ambitions are all on my back. They cannot look to my sibling in case I don't measure up!"

"I'm sure that is a nice challenge for you. I can't imagine you failing them on any way!"

"Easy for you to say! Anyway, I really do have a soft spot for a sister. I've seen sisters fight like cats and dogs, but in the end they hug and make up. There were times I found myself crying myself to sleep because I didn't have a sister."

"Kavita, don't forget there are no guarantees in life. Instead of a sister you could have had a brother or two!"

"Did you have to throw that in there? I guess I could have lived with a brother. From what I have seen they are not as much fun."

"I second that, but I put up with that little runt, and I already miss him."

There was a soft tap on the door, and the steward came in with cake. Kavita sang Happy Birthday as she lit the candle, told me to make a wish and blow it out. We moved back to the couch after enjoying the cake, and the steward handed us our champagne glasses.

The steward asked, "Is there anything else I can get you?"

She said, "No, we are fine. That will be all."

Through all this I had been working hard to keep my eyes off her prominent cleavage. We both took a sip out of our respective glasses, and my eyes drifted down. She put her glass down, lowered her gaze toward her breasts and pushed them upward with her free arm. She and did a shimmy that drew my eyes back to her cleavage. All the buttons snapped open as she took a deep breath while pushing her breasts together with her arms. She laughed nervously as they popped free. I put my hand on a breast and pulled her to me for a hug. She put her hand on top of mine, put her nipple between my fingers and started to massage and squeeze it. She was smiling broadly, and so was I. She locked the door and sat on my lap. I squeezed her behind, and she looked at me with raised eyebrows. She lifted herself to pull the skirt from under her, and I moved my hand to her bare behind. We undid the buttons of my shirt and her breasts felt like red-hot pokers as she pushed them against my bare chest. By this time I was fully aroused, and she did a shimmy against my erection. She had her face on my shoulder and I could hear her breathing hard. I'm sure she heard me doing the same. I had never held a woman like this and was giddy with pleasure. She was running one hand up and down my back and the other on my chest. I followed her example and ran my hand up and down her back. She was displeased, grabbed my hand and put it back on her breast.

She looked at her watch, and it was past the time for her to go. We were crushed, and I saw those voluptuous breasts disappear inside her blouse. During all this she had been rubbing her hips against me. We embraced one last time, and we had no choice but to walk out. Before we left I took a deep dish, put food in it and covered it with another plate.

She asked, "Just in case you get hungry later?"

"No. I didn't tell my friends about this dinner, and you know they'll have a thousand questions, but they won't believe a word of what I tell them. Then I'll spring this food on them, and they'll be on their knees begging for a bite."

"You are unbelievable. I knew you were a conniving type, but had no idea how bad you really are. I'll want details"

"Thank you. I do my best to keep you entertained. Anything else you have to tell me?"

"Yes, but now isn't the time."

She walked me to the entrance to my section, gave me a cursory hug and looked at me. I turned her sideways, hugged her and grabbed the breast on the side of the wall. She didn't react because she was too unhappy about the abrupt end to our dinner date. She had the shawl thrown over her shoulder, and I carefully arranged it over her shoulders to cover her cleavage. She gave me a weak smile and kissed me on the cheek. She made a sour face because all she got was my scraggly beard! She gave me a dirty look and slowly walked away. I stood there and watched her longingly. I watched her longingly as she disappeared around the corner.

I went up to the main deck for a walk because I was in no condition to face my friends. I needed to cool off from the dinner and the sizzling after-dinner encounter. Also I knew they wouldn't be happy about my missing dinner without telling them, and it was a very long walk back to my cabin. I put the dish outside the door before walking in. They were all waiting for me on my bunk, and it looked like an angry mob. They asked where I had been, and I told them I had dinner with Kavita. They asked how it went with her parents. I told them they weren't there—it was just the two of us. They were thoroughly shocked and wanted details.

"Her mother helped arrange the dinner for us. So we had dinner together."

That blew their collective minds. I didn't want to complicate matters by telling them about the birthday part of it because they might have lynched me. One of them said, "What do you mean her mother arranged the dinner? I thought she would be greeting you with a shotgun to protect her daughter from the likes of you!"

"That is where you are wrong. I'm sure she is a lovely lady and wanted her daughter to have a good time."

"Right! My name is Genghis Khan and I have a lovely dinner for you—*your liver!*"

"Alright, alright. I was not hungry and I wandered around the ship contemplating the end of this voyage. Is that more believable?"

"Poor Rajinder. He was on deck having a good cry because he's going to lose Kavita!"

"You are partly right. I did have a cry because we'll be parting soon. That was after a lovely dinner in a private dining room with the steward serving a wonderful Indian meal."

"Now we are sure you are lying because there is no Indian food on this ship."

"Yes there is. Just have to know the right person and be at the right place. Now if you will all excuse me I want to go to bed and dream about what all happened while I was crying on deck."

"Yeah, yeah, yeah. Tell us more stories we might believe."

I raised my hand and held up my index finger—telling them to wait. I brought in the dish from outside, removed the cover with a flourish and showed it around. There was dead silence as they inhaled the delightful aroma of Indian food permeating the cabin. I put it on the table and told them to enjoy 'my crying on the deck'. They were orderly as they each took a taste, and enjoyed the morsels they got. Then they did a collective genuflect and apologized for doubting me.

"I forgive you all, my sons. Now leave me in peace to enjoy my reliving of that dinner and the evening. Good night."

They walked out in silence with their heads bowed. My cabin-mate, Mohan was sitting on his bunk taking it all in. He was a quiet type and hadn't been talking much. Also he was ten years older than me, and he was on his way to a new job in Germany. Now he had questions about Kavita and seemed genuinely interested.

I asked, "Why didn't you ask me before?"

"I figured it was your business. I was definitely curious, but by now you should know I'm not the talkative type."

"Yes, I gathered that."

"I try to mind my own business, but my curiosity got the better of me. So how is it between you two? Looks to me it is serious."

"Mohan, it is wonderful between us, and it is serious. I'll anticipate your next question—will we see each other after we leave the ship? That is unknown. We are both going to America, and she tells me she will come see me in Indiana. That would be wonderful, but I don't see how she'll be able to get away from her parents."

"That is an exciting prospect, and I sure hope she comes to see you. I've seen you two together and looks like you have something very special. She is very enamored with you, and it seems you are with her."

"You are very observant. What a stroke of luck she noticed me and is interested in me. I'm barely hanging on during this ride because I have no experience with women."

He was sympathetic. "We are all in the same boat as far as experience is concerned. Seems to me you are doing fine. Just be yourself and you can't go wrong."

"Thank you, Mohan. She's been sweet to put up with my rambling and bumbling ways."

"I don't know about that. Has she been smooth and polished? I doubt it. More than likely she has no experience either and might be having the same talk with someone right now."

"You may be right. This is her third voyage, and I figured she'd be smooth and polished, as you put it. More than likely she is also winging it, and I'm unnecessarily worried."

He continued, "The other thing you have to consider is our norms in India. I'm sure she has not been involved with anyone before because it's just not done, and I'm not sure how she was able to pull this off. What confuses me thoroughly is her mother arranging this dinner for you. Have you met her mother?"

"No. I haven't, and you are not the only one confused. I was apprehensive about the dinner. First I thought we would be in the dining room with her parents. I was afraid they would have read me the riot act and have the steward march me back to my cabin. What a relief when we were in a private dining room. Still, I half expected her mother and father to come barging in. I was reassured by Kavita being very relaxed through it all."

"Sounds like you have her mother's support, which is unbelievable. Did she say anything about how her father might be thinking?"

"She has not, and I'm afraid to ask. I can't see how she would be able to come see me in America without him knowing. She's a wonderful woman, and I'm so very lucky to be with her. Oh well, maybe I'm seeing too much in this and getting too far ahead of myself."

"You are putting it mildly. The actual statement has 'head over heels' in it. I think she is right there with you on that."

"You may be right, and it has been quite a ride. I've not felt like this before, and I'm really dreading Genoa."

"I fully understand. I'll make myself scarce if you want to use the cabin. I should have made this offer earlier, but you know me—the least talkative guy of the group."

"Thanks, Mohan, that's very nice of you. I'm not sure how that would go over with the gang. Time is getting short and we will bumble through the rest of the trip. I really appreciate this offer and talk."

"Just one last question. How was the dinner?"

"It was a very sumptuous feast. We had champagne, and I'm a little woozy from that."

"That's pretty fancy stuff. I've heard about champagne, but never had any. You are a lucky guy. I would give anything for an Indian dinner right now because this Italian food just doesn't measure up."

With that we called it a day. I went to sleep with a very broad smile on my face enjoying the thoughts about the food and Kavita. Well, mostly Kavita!

Crossing the Suez Canal was interesting and took a better part of the day. Kavita and I managed to be together for part of the crossing. Being with her was wonderful, and we enjoyed the sights. We were at the railing, and she was pressing her body hard against me.

She said, "Nice canal, but we would have had a lot more fun if we had to go around the Cape of Good Hope!"

"Your wish did come to pass, but few years ago."

"What do you mean 'Came to pass, but few years ago?'"

"You don't remember the war over Suez Canal a few years back?"

She looked at me quizzically. "What war a few years back?"

"That was when the Egyptians nationalized the canal, and the British, French and Israelis launched an attack. I'm sure there was ingrained racism involved, and the colonial powers had a sense of entitlement with the thought, 'How dare they do this. We'll show them who's the boss!'"

She looked at me admiringly and said, "I vaguely remember something like that. You know what happened?"

"Yes, it was quite a hubbub at the time."

She interrupted me and asked, "How is it you know that much about the war? How old were you at the time—fourteen?"

"A couple of reasons. I had an English tutor because my language skills left a lot to be desired. One thing he emphasized was for me to diligently read the Editorial page of the newspaper. He said the English was very good, which should help me a lot. The second reason was the debate in my high school."

"You had a debate in your high school? Which side were you on?"

"I was too junior to participate in the debate, but I was rooting for Egyptians against the colonial occupiers. From what I remember a majority of the students and debaters were with me."

"Reading the editorial page helped you on this subject?"

"Yes, it did. I don't recall all the details, but I remember aggression being excoriated. Also the Russians were rattling their sabers rather harshly and threatening a nuclear attack against the aggressors. The Egyptians scuttled a bunch of ships in the canal, which rendered it unusable."

"I would have remembered a wider war. It must have been settled because canal is wide open."

"Yes. I don't recall all the details, but I vaguely remember something about U. N. Security Council intervening at the behest of Americans. I'm sure that brought the hostilities to a screeching halt and the aggressors withdrew. I wrote to the Egyptians to clear the canal immediately because we would be needing it for our trip. As you can see they obeyed my command and here we are."

(See the Appendix for more details on war over Suez.)

"Oh, you! How impossible can you get?"

I interrupted. "You ain't seen anything yet."

"Oh, yes. Can't wait to hear what else you'll take credit for!"

"Well, give me time. I'm only nineteen and I can't solve all the world's problems in one fell swoop. You remember the expression 'Rome wasn't built in one day.' They had multitude of workers and soldiers, but here it's only three of us."

"What 'three of us'? What other dummies have you managed to corral to help you?"

"The three of us: me, myself and I!"

"I should know better than ask stupid questions. I don't know why I keep falling for all your antics."

"I don't know. Why do you?"

We arrived at Port Said, and a lot of peddlers clambered aboard to set up their wares. They had very fascinating displays, and I enjoyed perusing through all their wares although there was no way I could purchase anything. The reason being I was flying out of London, and I couldn't add even half a pound to my luggage! A few of us youngsters got off the ship for a stroll through the bazaars and sample the local cuisine. I also mailed a postcard to Daddy. On my return to the ship I found a letter from him on my bunk. He hoped I was enjoying my voyage. His short trip back to his base was enjoyable. Here is what he said about being quiet at my departure:

"I'm sure you noticed I was quiet and morose while others were having fun throwing flowers and garlands to the passengers onboard the ship. That was to be expected because a member of our small family was leaving for four to five years. That was bound to put me in rather a depressed mood, and I felt a bit down. I hope you didn't mind."

He asked about the ship's routine and the food on board. He wished me a happy journey and hoped to hear from me soon. (Full letter is in Appendix.)

I met Kavita later, and she wanted to know what I was so pleased about. "I'm so very happy to see you, and I'm glad it shows."

"Quit goofing around, and tell me what this is about."

"I just received a letter from Daddy."

"What do you mean just received a letter from Daddy?"

I showed her the letter, and she was mesmerized. "I'll let Daddy know about being able to receive letters along the way. That would be wonderful."

"Maybe he knows and just hasn't told you."

"That is possible, but I don't think he knows. In business it would be useful to get letters along the way."

"Yes, it would. What business is your Daddy in?"

"Custom designed electrical drive systems with emphasis on high power motors. Don't ask me what that means. Do you know what that means?"

"To a certain extent. Sounds pretty interesting."

We went for a cup of tea, and Kavita asked, "You still have me intrigued about your being at the boarding school. I know you had a very good education there, but there must have been more going on with you that would explain how you are today."

I gave her a surprised look and said, "I'm not sure what you mean. How am I too different than others of my age?"

"Trust me, you are different. You are very self-assured, which is something I haven't seen in men of your age. Remind me, are you nineteen or twenty seven?"

"Kind of you to say that! Although around you I feel all of fifteen!"

She was not pleased by that comment, "Will you stop reminding me I am older than you? What am I saying? In our culture that gives me the upper hand."

"Yes. Also they say, 'Age before beauty.' You win on both counts!"

"You know, you're really getting to be a pain." She paused for a second. "What am I saying? I like winning on both counts. Besides, let's talk about what I saw when I came out of the elevator on our first day on the ship. The other guys were being normal kids toward me, but you did nothing of the sort, which really intrigued me. I half expected you to come running, get down on one knee and insist I marry you!"

"Yes, and that's exactly what I did, but I don't remember if you said yes."

She looked at me in disbelief. "You are putting me on. You did nothing of the sort."

"Yes, I did. Unfortunately you had left by that time. Not my fault you are the impatient type. Lucky for you I came along walking behind you, otherwise we'd have stayed strangers!"

"Oh, you are impossible! Actually this exchange is a perfect example of what I mean when I talked about your stay in the boarding school. What more can you tell me about your activities there?"

"Yes, we had activities to broaden our horizon. We had various educational movies on-site every other Saturday night. For commercial movies we went to the movie theater."

"That sounds interesting, and reinforces what I was talking about. What else do you remember about your days there?"

"Now that you ask, yes there was something very interesting."

Warily she asked, "And that was?"

I snickered, "I fully understand your being wary! Just remember I have a reputation to uphold, and I'm glad to be living up to that! Anyway, we had a British theater company set up camp at our school for a week and they presented Shakespearean and other plays."

She looked at me in utter disbelief, "What? They set up the stage in your school? And it was a British troop?"

"Yes. Every evening they presented one or two plays. A lot of it was over my head, but it sure piqued my interest and a good kick in the pants to read more."

"And how did that go? Did you read Punjabi books or English ones?"

"Both. During my college years I managed to find a bookstore that allowed me to rent books at one rupee each." (About a dime each.)

"Wow. Sure beats buying the books. Any particular books you were interested in?"

"Yes. The troop goaded me to read the complete works of Shakespeare. Also reading Shakespearean play, Julius Ceaser was the class project during high school."

She was very intrigued. "What other books did you read?"

"Kon Tiki Expedition by Thor Heyerdahl was the book project during first year of college."

"What was that about?"

"Thor was visiting the South Seas Islands and was curious about where the population originated. For some reason he was convinced they came from South America and went about trying to prove South Americans could have traversed the four thousand miles using a raft made out of balsa wood. Those rafts were common in South America and he had one built with a small cabin on top. He set sail with a small crew and made it to Polynesia relatively unscathed."

She was surprised. "So he proved the islands were inhabited by South Americans."

"No, he didn't."

"Didn't you say he made it to the South Seas Islands?"

"He did, but that didn't prove the people came from there. He just proved they could have originated there. Another successful expedition needs to be mounted from Asian side and make a similar claim. For proof there has to be an exhaustive study of the population looking for similarities in language and culture."

"That sure complicates the process. It must have quite an adventure for Thor and his crew. Anyway, what else did you read?"

"I also read Erle Stanley Gardner's Perry Mason books. It was interesting how Perry doggedly pursued every lead to find the murderer with the help of his trusty investigator, Paul Drake. I tried to follow the twists and turns of his investigation, but was never able to guess the culprit. They were very absorbing books. I also read Tess of the d'Urbervilles by Thomas Hardy, and Pride and Prejudice by Jane Austin. I also read Punjabi novels."

She was surprised. "You read complete works of Shakespeare and all the other books you mentioned? That Shakespearean company really piqued your interest! Before you ask—compared to you I'm an igno.... What's the word?"

"Is this a trap or you really don't know the word ignoramus?"

"Yes, that's the word—ignoramus."

"You can call yourself anything you want, although I'm not sure why you would go there because you do have a degree."

She asked, "What else have you been up to that I should be aware of?"

"You mean all that reading isn't impressive enough? How could you have guessed I would have more up my sleeve?"

She looked at me and smiled, "Just a hunch. You don't seem to be the type who would sit around twiddling your thumbs."

"You are dead-on there—I'm not. I built radios."

She gave me a very amused look. "Come on, keep it in believable range."

"You mean reading all those books by a nineteen-year-old should have been enough?"

"No, silly, but building radios?!"

"Okay. I figured you would be skeptical. I want to show you something. I'll be right back."

I went to my cabin and did some rummaging through my suitcase. I picked up the picture I was looking for, came back and put it in her hands. It was the picture of the Marconi Radio Club at the college along with the Physics professor and the Principal. She was blown away.

I said, "We were busy at the college and worked on various electronics circuits to learn their operation. I'm sorry I don't have a picture of the lab because none of us could afford a camera. I was lucky to have an electronics whiz as a neighbor, and I built the radios under his guidance."

"You said you built radios—as in plural."

"Yes, I did. Friends and family members found out about that, and they wanted me to build radios for them. I had to put an end to it because it was interfering with my studies."

"Wow. That must have been something. You are quite accomplished for a nineteen-year-old!"

"Actually, building radios was child's play compared to the really big project."

She almost shouted, "What!?"

"I'm not sure I should tell you because you had trouble believing I built radios."

"What could be a bigger project than that?"

"I built a radio transmitter."

"Now you are really trying my patience. I don't know anything about radio transmitters, but I do know only big companies build those things. I can't envision anyone building one—let alone a nineteen-year-old!"

I gave her a combative look, "Didn't you mean to say an average nineteen-year-old? Actually I was eighteen at the time. "

MARCONI RADIO CLUB
D. A. V. COLLEGE, AMRITSAR.
SESSION 1959-60.

The Principal is third from left. The Physics Professor is to his left and I am next to him

35

"In other you were not an average eighteen-year-old?"

"Do I really need to answer that question?"

She gave me a rather exasperated look, but that soon turned to an adoring one. "I'm sorry, Rajinder. So how was it that you built a transmitter?"

"My college was having an open house and a lot of projects were being proposed. I told my mentor, Mr. Rishi about it and asked if he would like to come visit. He asked if I was presenting anything. I said I was not, and he commented, 'Yes, you do now.'

"I gave him a puzzled look, and he said, 'You are going to build a transmitter.'

"I laughed and said, 'Good one, Mr. Rishi. I'll do that right after I come back from the moon.'

"He wasn't laughing. 'You finished with funny remarks? This is a simple project. I give you a circuit, you build it, I'll fine tune it, and you'll have a working transmitter. It's just like when I trained you to build radios. Are you game or am I wasting my time with you?'

"I was confused, but said, 'Since you put that way, how can I refuse? I'm ready whenever you are.'

"He gave me an approving look, 'That's more like it. I'll have a circuit and parts list for you in the morning. In the meantime, get your work area cleaned up to make room for this project. From what you told me you have no time to waste.'

"I snapped to attention and said, 'Yes, Sir. Your wish is my command. I'll get right on it.'"

Kavita said, "So you built a transmitter. It must have been quite a hit."

"I talked to my Physics professor and he talked to the Principal. They liked the idea and paid for the parts. When it was finished I left a radio on the Principal's desk and broadcast from an adjacent building. He was blown away, and gave me a prime spot in the exhibit hall."

"That is great. Like I said, I had sensed you were different than others your age. Anything else you did before you hit the high seas?"

"Nothing of major significance. I built a record player out of scrap parts I had lying around. My allowance didn't allow me to buy one, so I had to improvise. It looked nothing like a real record player."

"You have been a busy little beaver, haven't you? Oops, ignore the *little* part!"

"Thank you. I was having trouble coming up with the motor to drive the turntable because most of them were too big. Finally I settled on a bicycle dynamo, which worked fairly well as a motor. It ran on six volts A. C. from my home-built radio. Dad was proud of that and had me play records for all visitors. They were blown away by my home built contraption."

Kavita was having trouble taking all that in. Apprehensively she said, "I'm afraid to ask—is there anything else you made or did?"

I snickered and said, "Yes, there is. I also built an oven. We didn't have one because those things were too expensive. I had a metal shop make me a small box. I added heating elements from clothes irons and had a working oven. I had no way to control the temperature. It would only reach three hundred degrees because there was no insulation on the box. It did fine for baking small cakes and other minor confections. Before you ask, no, there's nothing else!"

"Wow, I'm breathless just listening to all you did by age of nineteen. And the degree is huge topper. Compared to you I've been goofing off all my life."

"No, Kavita. You have a degree, which you don't get if you had been goofing off. It's just that I am a very curious person and like to build things. It has been a very adventurous few years and I'm looking forward to more after I get to America."

"I can see that coming. I have a feeling you will do well there."

"Thank you, Kavita."

I saw her following day, and we were talking about the letter I received from my father. She said, "My father was pleased to learn he could receive letters along the way."

I looked at her mischievously, "And did you tell him where you got that information?"

"You are hilarious. He is liable to kill you, but he wouldn't harm his only child."

"That's great, Kavita. You are a heroine in his eyes. Isn't that wonderful?"

She was pleased, "Yes, and thank you for telling me."

"Don't mention it. I'm glad to help keep you on the good side of your father. If he finds out about me, you can tell him I was the one who told you about the letters. It might save my life."

She was upset by this comment. "My father is not a violent man. He wouldn't hurt you."

"Didn't you just say he is liable to kill me? Now which one is he?"

She ignored that question. "Where will you be staying in Indiana?"

I gave her the address and telephone number of my friend I would be rooming with.

"What about flights to Indiana?"

I showed her my airline tickets, and she made notes.

"I'll see if there is any way I can come see you in Indiana."

"Kavita, I seriously doubt your parents will let you take off on your own!"

However, she was quite a headstrong girl, and I had a feeling she could get her way regardless. Our involvement was a perfect example of her being different than most Indian girls. She noticed me when we were boarding the ship. I must have intrigued her because I was the only young Indian man taller than her. Any other girl might have just left it at that, buy not Kavita. She sought me out. In any other place that would have been difficult, but on the ship it was not too hard. All one had to do was look on the main deck. Initially she must have checked in the first class section. She came looking in the economy section when she didn't see me there. Even then it was not simple because there was the complication of my being with my friends when she first saw me. She couldn't just walk up to me, say hello and walk off with me. Her persistence paid off when I came walking behind her. She didn't just say hello and wait for me to say something. She introduced herself, turned around and walked with me. In other words, she saw something she liked and went after it.

From Port Said the ship headed to Naples, Italy. The Mediterranean Sea was living up to its rough and tumble reputation, and I was seasick. The ship's doctor gave me pills, and I slept the rest of the day. I was a bit groggy when I woke the following morning because my stomach was still not fully settled. I was also ravenously hungry because I had missed most of the meals the previous day. I saw a note from Kavita dated the previous day. She had come looking for me, and she had sent a note when she didn't see me on deck. That concerned me, and after breakfast I went up to the deck. She gave me a stern look and wanted to know why I had ignored her. I told her about being seasick and sleeping most of the day. My being unwell concerned her and asked how I was doing. I told her I was still a bit woozy, but was functional.

We arrived at Naples, and she went ashore with her parents. I went ashore with my friends, and the Italians were fascinated with my turban and full beard garb. I tried to find starch for my turbans, but no shopkeeper spoke English, and no one volunteered to translate. I was surprised by that because this was a major international port and one would assume they would have someone speaking English. I didn't think of asking the crew on board the ship for help.

Later that evening I saw Kavita. "I have a present for you, Rajinder. I want you to promise you'll use this pen when you write to me. Here is my address in India."

"Kavita, I'm really touched. I'm sorry, I didn't think about getting you a gift." Oh well, what can you expect from a nineteen-year-old kid! I was too busy trying to find starch for my turbans.

We talked about America. She said. "I'm definitely coming to see you in Indiana."

"Please don't get my hopes up. Have you told your mother about me?"

During our talks I had understood she was very close to her mother and told her everything.

"No, I haven't told her about you in particular. She did arrange the dinner for you the other night. I'm not sure how she would feel about my coming to see you."

"Then how do you expect to come to Indiana? You just can't take off without telling your parents. Please promise me you won't do that."

Reluctantly she promised, and I was surprised she was even thinking along those lines because that could cause a huge rift between them. I just didn't want to be the cause of the rift.

She said, "We need to get ready for the morning debarkation. I'll be able to meet you if we get everything packed."

Luckily she had time for us to say good-bye. We went to the secluded place she had found earlier, and we were both very broken up about parting. We stood silently leaning over the railing and looking out into the darkness. She moved closer and we embraced. She pressed her cheek against mine, and we held each other. It was hard to imagine how close we had become over the two weeks on the ship.

She said, "I will see you in Indiana. You can count on that."

"That'll be absolutely wonderful. I'm really looking forward to seeing you again."

She was very teary-eyed, "I will write to you from London."

I was also in tears. "I'd really like that a lot. I don't like the fact I won't be able to write to you. I don't like that at all."

"I'll telephone you when we arrive in America. It'll be wonderful talking to you again."

Our parting was very difficult. We were saying, "I'll miss you!" over and over again as we held each other. She had her face on my shoulder, and I could feel her tears. I also had tears running down my cheeks. She was sobbing silently, and I did what I could to console her. Slowly she calmed down and we pulled back to look into each other's eyes. I wiped her tears and wondered if she wanted me to kiss her, but I didn't see her purse her lips. Also she had taken the lead all through our relationship. We had little choice but to slowly walk back. We embraced one final time before heading to our respective cabins. I slept fitfully because I was tossing and turning, and the night dragged on and on. I was bleary-eyed and exhausted when I stumbled out of my bunk in the morning. I didn't have time to fumble around because I had to get ready to disembark. Mohan saw my eyes and was very sympathetic. He stayed close to make sure I got off the ship safely. I saw Kavita leave with her parents. She turned to wave, and I waved back. I watched her as she disappeared into the crowd. "Hope to see you again, Kavita," I murmured under my breath. Time will tell.

I was a bit unsteady on my feet, and Mohan was helpful. He was shorter than me, but he was strong. We got off the ship and found our way to the railway station. It was an enjoyable train journey through Italy and France. He got off the train in Paris, France, and I was sad to see him go. I was doing better, but it would have been nice to have him along to London. My distraction was gone, and was feeling down again. I busied myself by making notes in my journal. Once again I had to contend with something new—French food. This was a bit of a challenge, but it was just for the day. 'Do not drink the water' signs were all over the place, and only bottled water was safe to drink.

I arrived in Calais, France and took the ferry across the English Channel to Dover. The sea was rough—almost as bad as the Mediterranean Sea, but the ride was relatively short, and I didn't get too seasick. From Dover it was another train ride to London. The hotel had dinner waiting even though I was late arriving. I was bone tired and slept very well. Next day I found an Indian restaurant. What a treat. The last Indian meal I had was on the ship with Kavita and before that in Karachi. I had three days in London, and the anticipation of seeing Marina kept my mind occupied. I spent the time catching up with my journal. Also I watched television in the lobby. That was fascinating because I had not seen television before. I didn't understand any of the Christmas programming, but it was interesting. Later I had dinner at the hotel restaurant.

Marina didn't arrive, and I was feeling very down when I went to bed. She might have been delayed, and I was sure she would show up the following day. I had a very restless night and dreamt about being with Kavita on the ship. We hugged and slowly walked away with our arms outstretched toward each other. I woke with a start and had trouble going back to sleep.

The following day I decided to go sightseeing because I didn't want to sit around the hotel waiting for Marina. I left word at the front desk about her, and let them know I would be back by two in the afternoon. The staff gave me a list of places to see and a map of bus routes. I was on my way to see Big Ben when I saw a Gurdwara (Sikh temple). I got off the bus at the next stop and walked back to pay my respects. I was really surprised to find a Gurdwara in London and enjoyed talking to the priests and other congregants. They could tell I was fresh off the boat and asked where in England I was headed. They were surprised to hear I was on my way to America and this was just a short stop on that long journey. They asked me what I was doing in London. I explained about my German pen pal and this being the perfect opportunity to meet her. Most of them were Daddy's age and were absolutely blown away by my story. One of them wanted to know if I was going to marry her. I told them I had not thought about it because she was just a very good friend, and we had been corresponding for six years. They had trouble taking that in, and couldn't envision a woman as a friend.

I arrived at Big Ben, and the size and stature of the clock just blew my mind. It struck eleven shortly after I arrived there, and I couldn't believe how loud it was. I walked around taking in the sights and wanted to see Westminster Abbey, but the line was too long. I had lunch at a sidewalk cafe and took a slow walk to absorb the atmosphere. I got back to the hotel, but there was no sign of Marina. I wrote her a letter expressing my concern and hoped everything was all right with her. Now I had two things on my mind—Kavita and what happened to

Marina. It was almost more than I could bear, and I had another rough night because I had never felt that down and alone before. It never occurred to me to get Marina's telephone number before I left India. Later I learned her father had passed away at the time and she couldn't get away.

On December twenty-fifth I had my introduction to Christmas—there were no cabs available to take me to the airport. The hotel sent one of their staff members to drop me off. It was a long flight to New York. The four piston engines were extremely noisy, and I could feel the vibrations. I enjoyed the flight regardless and spent time catching up with my journal. I was very tired from not sleeping well the previous few nights, but I slept sporadically because of all the noise and vibrations. We had to stop in Bangor, Maine for gas before proceeding to New York. The customs agent asked me where I was headed. I told him I was taking an afternoon flight to Indiana, and he wanted to know what I would be doing until then. I told him I would like to tour the city. He looked at this nineteen-year-old youngster and just didn't like the idea of my fumbling around in New York because I would be an easy prey for all kinds of mischief. He talked to another agent, and they arranged for me to take an earlier flight. For a nineteen-year-old it was an order, and I concurred.

I wanted to sleep for twelve hours because I was bone tired, but the flight to Cleveland was not very long, and my seatmate had lots of questions. I didn't have the heart to tell him I wanted to be left alone. In Cleveland I changed planes for Fort Wayne, Indiana and also let Ranjit know I would be arriving earlier. By this time my tiredness really showed, but the flight to Fort Wayne was also short so there was not much time to nap. The stewardess noticed and brought me extra strong coffee. Later she stopped by to talk to me. On learning I was from India, she said that was one country she would really like to visit. I offered to escort her there after completing my studies in America. She gave me her telephone number, and I gave her mine. We chatted for a few minutes, and then she had to take care of her duties.

I arrived in Fort Wayne, Indiana on December twenty-sixth. My friend, Ranjit was waiting with a friend who had a car. This journey began in northern India on the second of December and then out of Bombay on the eighth.

Chapter 2

Indiana

Journal Entries

<u>December 27</u>

It was nice seeing my friend, Ranjit at the airport, and he was happy to see me. I gave him a letter from his parents, which was dated November twenty seventh. He commented how slow the delivery was, and I told him I would make sure it would be quicker the next time around. Besides, what did he expect for free special delivery! We laughed and headed to the car. It was an eerie sight because everything was covered with snow. The streets were mostly clear, but driving was rather hazardous. More than once the car slid sideways, but the driver knew how to handle it under these conditions. That didn't mean he wasn't nervous when it did something unexpected.

We arrived at a cozy upstairs one-bedroom apartment and talked about my trip over a cup of tea. Ranjit had traveled the same route the previous year and asked why it took me three days longer. I explained about my stop in London where I was hoping to meet my pen pal, Marina. He was surprised and wanted to know why I hadn't mentioned anything about her back in India. I told him it was not something I talked about because people would get the wrong impression about our six-year correspondence. I explained she was a very good friend and that was the perfect opportunity for us to meet. Unfortunately she didn't arrive, and I was very worried about her. He was sorry I missed seeing her, and she must have had a very good reason for not coming to London.

We talked about dinner, and he showed me the small kitchen. The landlady had provided a fully furnished apartment, and we had brought along spices and other ingredients. We both had learned to cook before we left India. I got busy cutting and chopping onions and vegetables while he got the rest of the ingredients together. After dinner we went downstairs to the landlady's patient waiting room to watch television. She heard voices and came to check and Ranjit introduced me. She was a short Russian doctor who worked out of the house. She was quite surprised I was so much taller than her. She left and we watched the television for a while. Soon we headed upstairs because it had been a very long day for me and I was bone tired.

The apartment was a short walk from college. The snow was deep, and it was very cold outside. Luckily we wouldn't be driving in this mess because we didn't have a car. I had a few days to settle in before registering for classes. Ranjit was studying Mechanical Engineering, and I was studying Electrical Engineering. He filled me in about the requirements as we looked over the schedule of classes, and the Orientation class was the first order of business for me.

December 28

Ranjit and I walked to the grocery store to pick up supplies. We had to carry it all back because we didn't have a car. We must have been quite a sight—a couple of turbaned men trudging through the snow and ice. We laughed it off and got back rather tired and very cold. I realized I needed a pair of gloves, but I had enough sense to bring along an overcoat.

I wrote a letter to my friend, Maldev letting him know I had arrived in Indiana and was looking forward to seeing him. I had met him in India at a small reunion of students from the boarding school. He was the elder brother of one of the students. He was visiting from California, and it was very interesting talking to him. We had taken to each other and spent quite a bit of time chatting. The other classmates were busy with their own routines and didn't pay attention. He spoke glowingly about his adventures in California and all the coeds he had at his disposal. He was coming to my hometown the following week, and I invited him to dinner. He was unable to do that, and we had settled for a couple of lunch meetings. He was very adamant I should join him in California, and we would have a jolly good time together. Unfortunately, I was unable to get admission to the college he was attending.

January 10

I went through Orientation and got the classes I wanted. Pretty soon we got down to the daily grind of classes, studies, cooking and some minor recreation of watching television downstairs in the doctor's waiting room. Sure saved us money on movies, which cost a whopping fifty cents.

January 12

Today I had a wonderful surprise in the mailbox—a letter from Kavita. She was missing me, and the journey to London was interminable. She missed our chats and walks, and she is really looking forward to seeing me again. Her mother, Meena was very excited when she learned about me. In her younger days she had a similar experience with a young British Army officer on her way back to India. He had gotten off the ship in Egypt. Kavita was stunned to hear this. Her mother was not sure her father would let her come see me by herself, but Kavita didn't want her parents along. She told her mother she was not a baby and reminded her it was her third trip overseas. Here she used me as an example. She said I was only nineteen and had traveled halfway around the world—alone. She recounted my itinerary, and her mother sat there wide-eyed. She couldn't imagine a mother letting her nineteen-year-old child take off to the other side of the world by himself. Meena's comment about my mother was, "She should be arrested," in a barely audible whisper.

Meena said she would talk to her father, but she was not sure how to explain Kavita taking off for Indiana. Her daughter going off to see a boy! Kavita told her mother I was not a boy. She asked her how she could call me a boy. She explained I had a Bachelor of Science degree, and had traveled halfway around the world alone. Reluctantly her mother agreed with her. Still she was not sure her father would let her take off for Indiana. In closing Kavita was adamant she would come see me, and I gave her full marks for being positive. I'm sure she knew how to get her way with her father. Once again only time will tell.

That was quite a letter from her, and she's a headstrong girl. I better get it right—woman!

January 16

I purchased a typewriter for college work, writing letters to Daddy and keeping up with my journal because handwriting everything was painfully slow. My English professor, Mr. Fox had no objection to my using the typewriter for homework and book reports. Luckily I had learned to type in India and was fairly proficient at it. The following is part of my letter to Daddy about my first couple of weeks here. I wrote to him using the new typewriter:

"Living seems to be much cheaper here when compared to Indian standards. Ranjit and I are living frugally by doing our own cooking at all odd hours because it is much cheaper than eating in the cafeteria. The only problem is we cannot get whole-wheat flour. Otherwise we get all the necessities, even curry powder that is especially made to impart Indian taste."

January 19

I have settled in pretty well and gotten a feel for this place and the college. Ranjit filled me in about the routines because he has been here longer. We have divided the cooking responsibilities, and it has been going fairly well. I'm glad we both learned to cook before leaving India, and our respective mothers worked pretty hard getting us trained.

Our daily routine consists of early morning classes, taking a nap (sometimes), cooking dinner, studying and, finally, sleeping. Somewhere in there we make time for relaxation and visiting friends. The college keeps me very busy because I've taken eighteen units. Some days it was just two hours of classes and six hours on Tuesdays, which includes four hours of drawing. All the professors are easily approachable, even the Dean of the College.

Indiana is in the grip of a very severe winter, and it is exceedingly cold. We have to muddle through because we haven't been in snow before. I went to find appropriate shoes, and the salesman was more than helpful. I also bought a pair of badly needed gloves.

I got a letter from Maldev, and he is moving along just fine in California. He said he was not sure who I was and why I had written to him. He had to sleep on it and finally remembered meeting someone in India that fit my description (Ha ha). He said he was also looking forward to seeing me. We had met in India on his visit there, and he was very helpful in getting me all the information I needed for coming to America.

January 27

We celebrated the Republic Day of India with great pomp, and there was a large crowd to see the variety show we presented. People were pleased with the program, and it was a great success. The forty students of the India Association worked hard to put on the show. My contribution was traditional clothing I asked Mom to send from India.

January 31

I wrote to Daddy about my routines and told him the college is only five days a week instead of six as it is in India. It is very cold here and the snow is piling up high. I sent him my photograph taken on the ship. Following is an excerpt from the letter:

"Here are some thoughts about this town. The people seem to be very nice and hospitable. Fort Wayne has three radio stations and three television stations. There are supermarkets and giant stores galore. You can see even a relatively small town has all these.

"Everything is proceeding smoothly, but there are no shops open on Sunday, and it is a bit of a challenge if we miss shopping on Saturday. We don't have any misgivings, and we take these things in stride by laughing at each other for not being on guard to pick up the requisites."

February 4

I finally got a letter from my pen pal, Marina. She was supposed to meet me in London but didn't arrive, and I was very worried about her. She said she would definitely have been there even if it were only two days to spend with me.

A year earlier she had to look after her father because of his illness and a couple of operations. Later he had surgery on his eye and was forbidden to drive, but he drove anyway. He crashed and was back in the hospital. During those days she had a tough time taking care of him, and last December he died of heart failure. That rapid succession of events could have broken anybody's spirit. That required great courage and a strong heart to recover from that tragedy. This was her first letter after the passing of her father, and she has mixed the news of her father's death with a sweet sense of humor. I had learned about her father's passing from Daddy. She had written to him because she didn't have my address in America. I had already written her a letter of condolence and prayed to God to give her the strength to bear the loss. I'm in awe of her courage and strong will that carried her through this tragedy.

February 6

A letter arrived from Kavita. She was still in England, and it was a short note to say hello and that she was missing me. She even included a hello from her mother, but she made no mention about her father, and it seemed to me they had not talked to him. This was quite frustrating because I was unable to write or talk to her. At least she can put something on paper and send it to me. All I had was this journal, but it was not the same because there was so much I wanted to tell her. Of course the big thing was that I missed her!

February 7

Saturday night we went to a cultural program at the Y.W.C.A., and the event was really enjoyable. There were Hawaiian dancers and dance music. It wasn't bad, but the fact remained I didn't know how to dance. Later we went for a cup of coffee. Sunday we had a very nice gathering of friends for lunch.

February 8

For the first time I had a strange feeling of loneliness today primarily because Kavita had been on my mind a lot. I hated to admit it, but I really missed her. I enjoyed her letter, which really lifted my spirits, and I was wondering how she was doing without any letters coming from me. She wrote that her friends were keeping her very busy.

I wrote to Marina to thank her for writing, and I really enjoyed hearing from her. I gave her a rundown of my routines here, and I kept it short because I've been very busy with college and housework. I worked hard to interject humor in the letter.

February 11

Kavita brightened my day with a birthday card. She had made my birthday very special on the ship, and this was the icing on the cake. She also included a letter with it. Oh how I wish I could write to her, but the only address I have for her is in India.

Also got a letter from Maldev. He is moving right along, and he asked when I was coming to California. He was looking forward to seeing me, and his main emphasis was 'no snow in California'.

Wrote a letter to Daddy, and I told him about my not receiving replies from relatives and friends in India. They had all extracted promises from me I would write to them from America, and it is exasperating not hearing back. The only letters I received were from him, Mom and Brother. Maybe I didn't get replies because the postage to America was so much higher.

The following is my comment to Daddy about my being in Sikh uniform:

"Being in the Sikh uniform (turban and full beard) is perfectly fine with me, although there are times some other Indians don't like it. Being in this uniform gives us some sort of distinction. When Americans are talking to a person from India, I might attract their attention if I was nearby, and they would start chatting with me. Those Indians do not come out and express their feelings openly, but they make no secret of their displeasure. Of course not all Indians are like that, just a small number from Bombay, and we try to stay away from them. Among the Americans we seem to be quite a curiosity."

February 15

The landlady said there was a telephone call for me, and I was trying to remember if I had given my number to anyone. I was quite stunned to hear Kavita's bubbly voice! "Hello, Rajinder. Guess who this is. How are you doing?"

"Hello Kavita. How absolutely delightful hearing your voice. I'm doing fine. How are you?"

"I missed you, but I'm doing great now that I'm talking to you."

"I missed you, too. How was your trip?"

"The trip was good but interminable. How is college treating you?"

"College is fine, and it keeps me very busy."

"That is great. Here, my mother wants to say hello."

"Hello Rajinder, this is Meena. It is very nice to talk to you. How are you doing?"

She put her mother on the telephone. My mouth went dry, and I was speechless because she said nothing to prepare me. Finally I found my voice and said, "Hello Mrs. Kapoor. I'm just fine, thank you. How are you?"

"I'm fine also, thank you. I just wanted to hear the voice of the guy who has my daughter fascinated, and you are all she talks about. What have you done to her?"

"I wish I knew. On the other hand I think of nothing else but her. She is the one who has me utterly fascinated."

"You have such a nice voice, and maybe that is what she really likes. She is nodding and smiling broadly."

There was a pause so Meena continued talking. "How are you getting along and how are your studies?"

I realized Meena was not going to berate me for sneaking around with her daughter on the ship. "I'm getting along fine and enjoying my stay. My studies are going great, and I like the college and the professors."

"That is great. Happy belated birthday and it was lovely talking to you. Here is Kavita."

She got off the telephone. I took a deep breath and wiped the sweat off my brow. Kavita was her bubbly self. "I can't believe how delighted she is having talked to you."

I heard her mother in the background, "Yes, I'm delighted."

"What did you tell her? Should I be worried or concerned?"

It was my turn to be mischievous. "Of course you should. You put your mother on without warning me. I blurt out things when I'm surprised like that."

"All right, what did you say to her?"

"That is between your mother and me, and I can understand why she is so pleased."

"Come on, you are not going to leave me hanging."

"You will have to ask her. Serves you right for putting her on without warning me."

"Look at it another way. Better I didn't tell you because it would have been much harder for you otherwise."

"You are probably right."

"Sure, I'm right. What did you tell my mother that she is so pleased?"

"Absolutely nothing. I was trying my best to keep from making too big an ass of myself and seems like I succeeded. I can't be held responsible if I blurted out something without realizing it. Other than that I think you are safe."

She was relieved, although she was still a bit apprehensive. "You must have said something. She was very pleased about talking with you and gave me quite a hug after handing me the telephone."

I thought about one of the letters I got from her and said, "Maybe it brought back wonderful memories about her being on the ship with that Englishman in her younger days."

"You might be right."

"All I know is I have missed you so much, and I really enjoyed getting your letters, but I'm not happy I couldn't write to you. By the way, thank you for the birthday card. That was the first card I ever received, and I will treasure it."

She was surprised. "I'm really surprised that was the first birthday card you ever received."

"Not only that, you are the first girl I've ever been involved with. I'm hoping you will be the first girl I'll kiss."

She laughed at my comment. "I find it hard to believe you have not kissed a girl."

From her conversation I could tell she could talk freely. "I have not kissed a girl because I had no opportunity. You know the morés in India. Just remember, you are the world traveler, and I figured you are the one with all the worldly experiences."

"You are sadly mistaken if you are implying I have been kissing men on my travels. Actually, I haven't been kissed either."

"Three world trips and never been kissed? Unbelievable!"

"I can't help what you believe. Besides, if I had been that type I would have kissed you because there were plenty of opportunities. I was hoping for my first kiss on the ship."

"Then why didn't you kiss me?"

She retorted, "Why didn't you kiss me?"

Our culture and upbringing held us both back. I said, "You know it is not done in our culture."

"I was hoping for a kiss during the good-bye embrace before Genoa."

"I didn't want to be too forward in assuming I could. I left it up to you because you had been taking the lead."

We had a good laugh. She said, "Just don't let another golden opportunity pass us by."

"I'll do my best. For that you'll have to be here because it is difficult to fulfill your wish with you there me here."

She asked, "Well, how was your meeting with Marina? Must have been very nice seeing each other after all those years of correspondence."

"Yes, it would've been nice."

"Oh, no! I don't like the sound of that."

"She didn't make it, and I was very worried about her. I knew something really bad must have happened because we were both very excited about the meeting."

"Yes, it must have been hard on you. Did you find out what happened?"

"She couldn't get away because her father had passed away. She wrote to my daddy because she didn't have my address here in America. I got the news from him after I got here, and I wrote her a letter of condolences. Later I got a letter from her explaining everything. She said she was really looking forward to spending a couple of days together after all those years of correspondence. She said disappointed didn't begin to explain how she felt."

Kavita was very sympathetic, "I'm really very sorry to hear that. I know it must have been very hard on you."

"Yes, it was a huge feeling of helplessness. I imagined all kinds of bad things that might have happened to her. She was a maniac behind the wheel and had been in a very bad accident, which laid her up for a couple of months."

"At least she was physically fine, but losing one's father can be very traumatic. I really feel for her."

"Yes. She has been a wonderful friend."

I heard her mother telling her to get ready for some function, and we got off the telephone. Talking to her mother had strengthened my hope about her coming to visit me. Kavita put her on the telephone to convince me she had her support.

I sat down and made some notes about the call. I was grateful my roommate was not there. I had not mentioned Kavita to him because I just didn't want to talk about it. I would deal with that if and when she had firm plans to visit.

February 17

Got a letter from Dad, and he was not happy about the shipping cost of traditional clothes I needed for the Indian Republic Day celebrations. He reminded me to anticipate my requirements so they could be sent by sea. He thanked me for sending my photograph, and he would send a copy to Grandmother. She was asking about me, and he reminded me to write to her.

Following is an excerpt from his letter:

"Your last letter was quite informative about the town, the climate and your day-to-day life. In fact your place is even colder than here, although your living conditions are more comfortable. Still it is always better to be a little careful about sudden exposure. I'm sure you are taking all the necessary precautions."

February 19

My twentieth birthday came and went without any fanfare. I was really hoping Kavita would be here, but that was not to be. Sometimes things are touted, and they seldom are what they are touted to be. Part of this also is I'm missing home. At this stage home is not one particular spot. Mom and Ravi are in Punjab, India while Daddy is posted in Kashmir. He is in a non-family station so Mom couldn't be there with him. She is in the process of packing to join him for the summer. I'm sure being with any of them at this juncture would have been wonderful. Kavita did her part making my birthday special on the ship, which was very nice of her and her mother. They really went all out, and I was overwhelmed.

February 21

The days have been running into each other. On top of that it has been snowing and it's really piled up high. Yesterday we thought the long winter was finally ending, but then we woke to find fresh snow piled up and more continuing to fall. Seems like we are in for another bout of bad weather. Winter might last till the end of March, which is really nerve racking, and there seems to be no end to falling snow.

I got a letter from Maldev, and he was kidding me about all the snowfall I wrote him about. His theme was, 'Not much snow in California—mostly some rain falling. Come to California, escape snow.' That really got me thinking of all the winters in India with not even a snowflake—ever. The longing for California was getting stronger.

So far Daddy's letters had been more of questionnaires except for the last one, which was nice for a change. Also I'll relate to him about a party thrown by the Faculty Women's Association for foreign students. That's where I met Mrs. Boriak who is quite a character and knew something about what we foreigners were up against. She took a special liking to me because I'm so tall and she is so short.

The topic of loneliness came up today. One of my Indian friends asked if I've been lonely and wished I were back at home. I don't have any such feelings, and it is difficult enough to stay levelheaded without these students coming around spreading their homesickness—almost like a calf pining for its mother. I don't know why they feel so lonely and downcast after having the resolve to come all this way. What a bunch of sissies!

I don't mean they shouldn't discuss the affairs with others, but they need to be tactful. It's easy to spread this infection, but extremely difficult to help the other person get over it. We can only say a few comforting words to the homesick person. We can't become his parent or family and have no way to provide what he might want or need—affection. Our capacity is limited to offering encouragement and telling him to be brave. It is all too easy to fall prey to loneliness. I don't mean to say I've never been homesick because I'm relatively immune and will be able to tide over these four or five years' stay without much difficulty. The five years I spent in boarding school (age seven to twelve) immunized me fairly well, and I won't be easily affected by this talk, but I do resent the discouragement they invoke.

We have been watching television in the landlady's waiting room. We make use of that once or twice a week. It is quite interesting getting familiar with various shows. The main ones we watch are "Rawhide" and "The Life of Riley". We didn't have television in India so this is a novelty and it sure saves money on movies.

February 22

Today I got a frantic telephone call from Kavita. They had received a cablegram from India informing them her grandmother had a heart attack and was in very bad shape. Her father telephoned home and learned she was barely hanging on. Her prognosis was not good, and the doctors said she might not last a week. She was asking for them—especially Kavita. Through sobs she told me her daddy was out getting airline tickets, and they would be leaving on the next available flight.

My heart sank at the news. I really felt very bad for her and what she was going through. I did what I could to comfort her, but failed miserably. Words got caught in my throat as I choked back my emotions. "Life is so cruel," she said through her sobs. She had to start packing and promised to post letters at every stop along the way. She promised to come back even if she had to walk. We said good-bye, and I sank onto the couch with my head in my hands. I was over-wrought at another good-bye, and I didn't even have a chance to hold her and comfort her. I had lost my grandfather two years earlier, and I really felt for her because I had a good idea what she was going through. I also understood how torn she must be feeling, not being able to be with me because she had to rush home to be with her grandmother. She was planning to come to Indiana with her mother, but that became a moot point.

That also hit me hard because I was so looking forward to seeing her again—even with her mother tagging along. All that threw me for a loop, and I was really depressed. I was feeling down and also feeling sorry for myself. There was no one I could lean on or look for sympathy, I just had to steel myself and carry on by burying myself in my studies and taking care of the small place we called home. It was not easy—but nothing ever is. Another woman I'm destined not to be with? My pen pal, Marina was to meet me in London, but she didn't arrive because she was dealing with the death of her father. Kavita has to rush back to India to deal with her grandmother's heart attack. Where is the justice in this? So is this what you call life?

February 23

I wrote to Daddy, and told him his last letter was wonderful—unlike earlier ones that were mostly questionnaires. I hoped future letters would be even more interesting than this one. I told him I had written to Grandma directly. I agreed with him about the cost of shipping the clothes, but the Republic Day function was coming up, and the traditional clothes would have arrived too late by sea. That was my contribution to the program the Indian Students Association was presenting.

I wrote to him about the heavy snowfall and how I was getting quite tired of it. I had never seen snow, and Indiana was having the heaviest snowfall in decades. It was the end of February, and there was no sign of spring. Luckily my overcoat was taking good care of me.

The following is an excerpt of my letter to Daddy about a party I attended:

"The other day we went to the party given by the society of the wives of the college professors. (Faculty Women's Association.) It was only for foreign students, and the professors were not invited. The President of the college was the only exception.

"It was a very interesting party, and we enjoyed talking to all the ladies present. Mrs. Boriak was the liveliest of them all. Just imagine the scene. She is hardly five feet tall in her high-heeled sandals and rather plump, and I am over six feet tall. She stood next to me and asked, 'How tall do I look?'

"This all added up to her being the center of attention and everyone had a good laugh.

"It's nearly three months since I arrived here, and the first term is coming to a close. We are kept very busy: classes, homework, housework, cooking, cleanup and washing clothes. Our usual sleeping time is one in the morning. We are up at seven to be at the college at eight."

February 24

Today there was an interesting discussion about sin in our English class. The professor, Mr. Fox said the state refuses to punish a man if he kills the enemy in battle, but the state could hold him punishable with death if he kills with any other intention. It took another turn when he talked about the wholesale destruction of the Japanese cities with the atomic bombs. He went on to say it was explained in the light of self-defense and to save American lives. Asked if it was a sin, he went on to say God didn't in any way consider American lives more important than Japanese lives.

I received a letter from Daddy. He had been concerned about my choice of major and was happy to learn I had chosen Electronics Engineering. This was something I was very interested in since I had built radios for friends and family. He was also happy I had written to Grandmother in the village. I had also told him about purchasing a typewriter, and he wanted to know if I could get a job as a typist. He also commented about my being in Sikh uniform:

"It has given me immense pleasure to learn you Sikh students are commanding greater attention of the Americans than other Indians. I really don't know why the majority of students choose to change their identity by shaving off. With the advantages you are getting I hope you will stick to the Sikh uniform. Of course at certain places you may be looked down upon, but there is nothing quite like maintaining one's identity and facing the challenges as they arise."

February 25

In his last letter Daddy wrote about his radio and its battery getting low. It was a tube radio I had built that was designed to run on a battery pack. His assignment was in a remote area, and it was not a family station. He was essentially camping out because there was no electricity. This battery-powered radio came in handy for him, and he enjoyed using it since I had built it.[3]

February 27

Over the weekend we were rather busy because we had some cleaning chores to do and catch up on studies. Some of the students were having a party, and we were invited. That was nice because we needed some excitement. It had been quite dull so far since it takes time to make new friends. All the Indians were newcomers here and didn't know anyone. Those get-togethers were the only way to meet other countrymen.

Recently I had a strange dream. Marina was trying to wake me. In that dream I woke and looked at her rather blankly. Perhaps I had been too fast asleep because it took time to fully get to my senses. I shook myself awake and almost shouted at her.

"Oh, hello Marina. Is it really you or am I dreaming?"

---

[3]   Those were the pre-transistor days in India

I had a sense of her presence near me even though I was seemingly asleep. I had no idea if I did shout in my dream, for there was no one around at the time. She sat down and gave me a heart-warming embrace with tears trickling down her cheeks. I had tears in my eyes and she wiped them after I had done likewise for her. She sat next to me, sort of reclining. We were silent and kept looking at each other for some time.

I said, "Isn't it strange, Marina. We meet for the first time in our lives after a long stretch of correspondence, and we elect to remain silent when the most pleasant wish of our hearts is fulfilled!"

She was silent for some time, and then said, "Yes, darling, and isn't it stranger still that silence should convey so much about our feelings toward each other."

She placed her lips on mine in a kiss. It is quite something how one small act can convey so many feelings, emotions and affection we bore for each other. Words seemed so inadequate in a situation like that. That kiss conveyed our deepest feelings we had for each other. It was then she broke down and sobbed. The last thing I remember was that I was sitting there comforting her. Why she was crying I do not know. I might one day figure it out.

March 2

"Faith is to believe what we do not see, and the reward of faith is to see what we believe." That is what I read today. I haven't followed its full implication. The second part of the phrase, "and the reward of faith is to see what we believe," is not clear to me, but I'm not concentrating on it either.

I like this quotation better, "Never delay kissing a pretty girl or opening a good bottle of whiskey. Both should be investigated as quickly as possible." This is from Hemingway. Too bad I didn't know about this saying on the ship!

March 3

We went to visit Jogi, another Indian student who had been here for three quarters. The conversation we had with him was not encouraging. Seems to me these old-timers try pretty hard to discourage the newcomers who are trying to get their bearings. I do feel they ought to put an end to this. The main theme of what he was warning us about was all the discrimination he had suffered. We really didn't understand what he was talking about because we had experienced none of that.

March 4

I received a letter from Kavita posted from London. She was very apologetic about leaving, but they just had to get back to her grandmother. She was all broken up because she couldn't come to see me. She was crying on the plane, and there were a couple of tears splotched on the letter. She absolutely hated how the airplane was so noisy and bouncing all over the place. She much preferred the ship where it was calm and serene, and she could move about as she pleased. She really enjoyed going ashore along the way. She missed me and was not happy there was no letter waiting for her in London like it would have been if she were traveling by sea. She was thinking how wonderful it would have been if she was going back to India and having a letter waiting for her at every port. Likewise she would have posted a letter to me at the same time. She knew air travel was the wave of the future, but all we could have done was said hello if we had been air travelers. She was bored stiff sitting on that plane for hours on end and was not looking forward to the rest of the journey.

I had posted a letter to her the day after her departure, and it might not get there before she arrived because letters to India were taking eight to eleven days. I was apprehensive about writing and wondered how she would explain it to her father. She said he didn't see all the mail because it was distributed by the servants and her letter would go directly to her room.

March 6

In my last letter to Daddy I had enclosed a clipping from the college newspaper, Nucleas. It was my photograph taken at the party given by the Faculty Women's Association, which showed how I towered above Mrs. Boriak. I still remember how she stood next to me and asked, "How tall do I look?" She was about five feet tall and the most jovial of them all.

I asked Daddy to order me a subscription to the foreign edition of Hindustan Times newspaper. Sure would be nice to keep up with news back home. I also told him about my plan to get an old short-wave radio so we could receive Indian radio stations because we are really missing Indian music.

I also recounted my visiting the home of Mrs. Shaw. She worked at the college post office and had invited us for dinner. Also present were their son, Lynne and his wife. They were asking about our turban and its significance. I explained we Sikhs didn't cut our hair, and the turban did a good job of hiding it. Lynne said, "I would be out of work if everyone followed your religion."

He was a barber, and we all laughed. I told him we were a small minority in India and his job was safe here. The dinner was very nice, and we had a lively conversation. One of us was a Christian, and he explained about the spread of Christianity in Southern India.

March 8

I got a letter from Daddy. It would be easier to quote him than trying to explain what he had to say:

"The account of the Faculty Women's Association party was exhilarating, and I feel proud you are making your mark with those who matter over there. You will have to be careful in two aspects:

"a) Never go in for cheap popularity.

"b) You must come up to the expectations of people who single you out.

"The above can only be achieved by a strong character and with solid knowledge of the subjects you are supposed to delve into. Put in a lot of study time in your college subjects. You must also include other subjects about India and our culture. I will order the newspaper for you, but that is not enough. In addition to your technical studies you must devote some time on additional subjects. In 1943 I met three Generals in Delhi. Two were British and one was American. They always made time to study because it was their daily habit. It didn't matter what time they came back from dinner outside or any other engagement. This habit has to be formed early and adhered to resolutely."

March 10

I just don't understand why laziness has crept into my routines for the last few days. Anyway, today was fairly pleasant, and later in the day I felt drowsy, but a cup of tea revived me. I had drawings to do for the Engineering Graphics class. I'm not good at this subject, but it is something I just have to learn. I was feeling down after spending hours on that.

After that I sat down to write in this journal. I am putting down all that comes to mind, things I dare not put in front of anyone else. I wonder who will get his or her hands on this. I would be happy if no one does because I don't feel good about anyone intruding into this part of my life. We all have our private lives into which outsiders are definitely not welcome.

That also raises the questions as to whether I would allow my future wife to go through this journal. I have not come to a decision, though I don't think I'd be able to stop her. Sometimes I feel a wife should not be allowed to have a peek into her husband's past life because it might bring up unnecessary suspicions. She could only go through portions when she came into his life. A careless remark could lead to a bad break and some of the worst headaches for both.

Then I feel everything should be open to her so this would lead to a better understanding of each other's thoughts and emotions. That might be helpful in married life and could explain some of the actions and behaviors of the individuals. Someday I might come to a decision on that point. 'Till then I will sit with my lips tightly shut on that subject.

March 12

I have been going for long walks here like I did in India where I was able to contemplate my thoughts, feelings and actions. It is hard to do that here because there is so much traffic and noise.

I was also thinking about Mom because she had something to say about love in her last letter. "I know how much you used to love me here.

You must be finding good consolation in loving the lady doctor as your own mother." I have no such feelings for the lady doctor, and we are avoiding her because she is easily irritated. I can't imagine her acting like that with her patients. Love for Mom is love for Mom, and no lady doctor or any other woman could take her place. I'm sure she is missing me, and that's her way of saying it. I miss her, too, and I will pass on my feelings to her.

March 14

In a letter to Daddy I talked further about the recent party. Most of it revolved around Mrs. Boriak. She was a very funny lady and was cracking a joke at every turn. I hadn't laughed that much since my arrival here. My being here is serious business, and I'm following the old adage, 'Nose to the grindstone.'

My first term is coming to an end, and we are in the midst of finals. After that we will have a week off. I have already signed up for classes and would be taking eighteen units. That would allow me to graduate in six quarters—2 years.

March 15

We went to see the movie "X-15". It gave us an insight into the development of famous speed-barrier crashing X-planes. Sometimes the pilots had to sit through hours of waiting while systems problems were taken care of. They were trained to be the very ideal of perfection because the slightest mistake on their part could very well lead to frightening consequences. Finally it was the teamwork that prevailed, and the results achieved were fantastic. It was exciting to see their work ethic, living through their agonizing moments and finally sharing their heights of achievements. That was quite an inspiring movie.

Got a letter from Maldev, and he was asking about my plans. I keep telling him there are no plans at this time, and any change would have to wait until after summer vacation.

March 21

It has been a long time since I heard from Marina. I wonder what's up with that girl.

I got a letter from Kavita. She had gotten back to India, and her grandmother was very happy to see them. Two days later she passed away. It was a very sad letter, and I really felt her pain. She said the funeral was very traumatic, and she could barely keep her eyes open. She wished I had been there to help her through it all. In the meantime she had received my letter, which really eased her pain. I had included my writing about Grandfather suddenly passing away two years earlier after a short illness. She thanked me for my comments and all the support. She was also very grateful for my being so understanding. Again she said she hated the plane trip and was glad it was over.

Reading through her letter was very hard. It brought back memories of my grandfather's passing.

Here is a part of the condolence letter I wrote to her.

"Kavita, it is with a heavy heart and deep sorrow I write this to convey my condolences about your grandmother's passing. I'm sure she was a wonderful lady, and you'll miss her tremendously. I'm also sure you'll cherish the wonderful time you had with her and gain strength from it. I'm very sorry I'm unable to be there for you to help you through this trying time. I am enclosing a copy of the essay I wrote at my grandfather's passing two years back."

Below that is what I wrote about my grandfather's passing.

Grandfather's Passing

This is the first time I've felt the impact of someone passing away. A few years back Mom's mother passed away, but I didn't feel much of an impact because I was too young. The passing of Grandfather had a profound effect on me.

We were at Daddy's sister's village to attend her daughter's wedding. My uncle from the village told us Grandfather wasn't feeling well and that was the reason he didn't make the trip. After the wedding Daddy went to the village to see Grandfather after dropping us off at home. He was not feeling well, but it was nothing serious. After a short stay Daddy came home. The following day we received a telegram from the village informing us Grandpa's condition had worsened, and Mom and Daddy left for the village following morning. I received a letter from Daddy saying Grandfather was still unwell but not in any danger. The next day they returned home because Grandpa was progressing satisfactorily. The following day Daddy took some more days off and went back to the village.

Later that evening I was in my room studying when the telephone rang. I answered, and the operator said it was a long distance call from Jaitu, a town near our village. On hearing that I prepared myself for the worst. I said hello, and recognized Daddy's voice.

"Hello Rajinder. Father died at six this morning."

I had read how people were speechless from sorrow, which always surprised me because I couldn't figure out how that could ever be. There I was—speechless. My mouth went dry, my knees buckled, and I collapsed onto a chair. Daddy was saying, "Father died....Hello, hello. Rajinder, did you hear me?"

At last I told him I had heard. He told us to come to the village and gave me instructions. Mom and I took the overnight train to Barnala, a town near the village where our driver was waiting with the car. I was speeding to the village on that miserable road, and the driver was getting uneasy. He asked me to slow down, but I kept quiet and carried on. On his fourth mention of slowing down I told him to just sit there quietly, and Mom told him to be quiet because I didn't like that kind of interference. After that he didn't speak.

Daddy was waiting for us when we arrived. I turned the car over to the driver and embraced Daddy tightly. I must praise his patience and self-control. I wept on his shoulder, and he did his best to console me. Then I went to see Grandfather, but I couldn't look at him. I sat to a side and wept bitterly. At about nine he was brought out for the final viewing. For the first time I looked at him.......

A big lump rose in my throat, but I couldn't turn my eyes away from his face. He seemed to be in deep, deep sleep, and only his spectacles were missing from his face.

Yes, that deep, deep sleep:

> From which he will never wake.
>
> From which he never will speak.
>
> From which he will never get up and walk about.
>
> From which he never will be seen on this Earth and all traces of him will be wiped away.

I watched him as he lay there. An irremovable curtain had snatched him away from our family circle. Soon he will be bequeathed to the fire and will be absolutely no more, and will never be seen again. What an irreparable loss. What an unbearable loss. Yes, I know. This was a loss that could never be prevented even if the whole world tried its level best....

"…. Rajinder."

I heard my name being called and was startled out of my reverie. Daddy wanted me to take pictures, and I did that. Soon we started for the cremation grounds, and I looked for opportunities to take photographs. He was taken to the Gurdwara (Sikh Temple) for his last respects, and we finally reached the cremation grounds. There he was bequeathed to the flames after a painful ceremony of prayers.

We came back home and sat there talking about Grandfather for quite some time. Daddy told us about Grandfather's father passing away when he was only fifteen and all the responsibilities of the family fell on his shoulders because he was the eldest son. He had tears in his eyes as he talked about how hard it must have been for Grandpa. Somehow he found the strength and the village rallied around him to make sure he was given the needed assistance. All that had to be a monumental task for Grandpa. As an adult he stood barely five feet tall and how he handled all the menial work at the tender age of fifteen is beyond my comprehension.

In his younger days Grandpa was basically an illiterate farmer because there was no school when he was growing up. That did not mean he was completely illiterate. He taught himself basic arithmetic and was able to read and write Panjabi fairly proficiently. He also saw the huge advantage of education and pushed to open a school when Daddy got to be five. It took some time and effort, but the village came together and school was opened a short time later. I was blown away by what I heard and my respect for Grandpa grew exponentially.

He was also a towering figure in the village. He rose to be the equivalent of a mayor and was very well respected even after he retired from that post. Daddy told us about all the people who came to the house to have their disputes adjudicated by Grandpa. He had no training of any kind, but let common sense and fairness guide him. Even I remembered a few cases of people walking into the courtyard asking for Grandpa's help. They would be very angry at each other and ready to come to blows, but they left satisfied with grandpa's verdict because they all knew he was very fair and impartial in his decisions. What was actually being discussed was beyond me, but I could see the changes in the persons' demeanor.

Later in the afternoon I left for home with Mom. Dad stayed behind to take care of Grandpa's affairs with his brothers and sister.

Rajinder.

To You Granddad, In Your Sacred Memory

The backbone of our family
*   that's what you were, Granddad*
Made brittle by the passage of time

Finally crumbled
*   on summons from the Almighty*
As you left us
*   heading for your heavenly abode.*

You left us at such a time
*   Granddad*
When your companionship
*   was vitally needed,*
And you left behind
*   your everlasting memory that*
*   will be unaffected by time.*

You left us at such a time,
*   Granddad*
When your valuable guidance
*   was so badly needed,*
Valued not just by family,
*   but also by the whole village.*

Yes, Granddad
*   the path for life you'd shown us*
*   will hold aloft the torch of guidance*
*   for the future,*
*   and be a constant source of*
*   inspiration for us*
*   for years and years to come.*

Your grandson,
Rajinder

March 22

We went to a very nice party last night. It was an enjoyable get-together, and most of the Indian students were there. The jokes tended to be racy, but I wouldn't say they were unpleasant. The party was actually in full swing when we arrived, and the beer was flowing freely. We enjoyed the food, and it was fun. Or—as much fun we could have without any girls present. There were no Indian girls at the college, and no one had acquired a girlfriend.

March 26

I received a letter from Daddy. He was happy to hear about our cooking routines and taking care of the apartment. He was commenting about how the Indian housewives were more proficient at complaining about the servants not doing the jobs to their taste, but not getting anything done on their own. He also said I should be a good cook by the time I graduated, and he liked my idea about getting a second-hand short wave radio. That way I would be able to catch the overseas broadcast bulletins of All India Radio and be able to receive the latest news from home. He also said he would arrange to send me various magazines. He liked the idea of my sending him the American edition of Reader's Digest.

March 27

The first term results are in, and I got a GPA of 2.94—just a hair under the 3.0 required to be on the merit list. In Math I got an A; Mechanical Engineering a D (not very good.); Engineering Graphics a B; History a B; English a B. Mechanical Engineering is not my strong subject!

I wrote to Daddy and passed on the results to him. I told him it was wonderful receiving Hindustan Times newspaper. I really missed reading it since I arrived here. Later I passed it to the college library.

March 31

I received a letter from Kavita, and she sounded much better. She would be going to college in the fall for her Master's degree. She thanked me for my letters, and said they really helped her a lot. What I wrote about my grandfather's passing really hit home. She had the same feelings about her grandmother's passing which helped her tremendously. She told me not to worry about her because she will work very hard to keep busy. Her letter was a bit short, her writing was rather poor and seemed like her heart was not in it. I understood her condition and wrote her a letter of encouragement.

Daddy had gotten over the initial worry and the feeling of my having gone from India. His first few letters were awful—tending to be just questionnaires, but his last letter was really wonderful. What I found striking in his letter was his, 'Yes, you should.' attitude. I asked him about getting a radio, and he told me to go ahead with the plan without delay. I asked him if he could send me some magazines, and he said he would be arranging them for me. I asked him if he would like copies of the American version of Reader's Digest. He would be waiting for them impatiently. I don't know what's up with him.

Ranjit has been depressed, and I decided to help him out by letting him escape from the usual humdrum of housework. I'll give him more time, and hopefully he will feel better soon. What could be bugging him?

April 2

My second term is in full swing, and this term classes start at nine, five days a week. Last term I missed some classes because I overslept. The problem was we were studying until one in the morning. For the new term the classes would be nine to one every day—much easier to handle than being scattered all through the day.

My take regarding Ranjit being depressed: it's funny how that coincided with our results from the last term. Could it be is doing poorly? He hasn't said anything, and I'm afraid to ask.

Still no letter from Marina. It has been a long silence, and I don't know what to do.

I got a letter from Daddy. He was with Mom in Amritsar, Punjab and they were in the process of packing for her move to Kashmir for the summer. He was complaining about how much stuff had been accumulated over the previous four years, and he was missing my being there to help. My brother Ravi was busy with his studies and was less than helpful. Daddy would write again after their arrival in Kashmir.

He was happy to see my results from the first term. He was sure I would be included on the merit list. That was unlikely—GPA needed to be at least 3.0.

Here is what I wrote to Daddy about my being a good cook after I graduate:

"You have quite a point about my cooking abilities. I'm wishing I better not be a good cook by the time I graduate. It is perfectly all right in my present situation, but it just won't do in the future married life. I don't feel good imagining my being in the kitchen doing everything while my wife is seated comfortably in the living room with her feet on the table and a novel in her lap while she calls out to me, 'Honey, is dinner ready?' It just won't do. Blessed are those with no knowledge of cooking!"

That last part includes Daddy! I'm pretty sure he would be lost in a kitchen!

April 4

A few days back I ran into Khanna, a close friend from the boarding school. We were classmates in the fifties, and we have been getting reacquainted after years of separation. We have been talking late into the night catching up with each other.

In India we used to listen to Radio Ceylon, which was a commercial radio station that used to broadcast popular music to India. Commercial stations were banned in India. Radio Ceylon was very popular because it played top-forty music, which we missed here in America. I told Khanna about fixing up an old radio so we could receive broadcasts from India. He looked at me blankly and couldn't figure out how that could be done. I told him that was pretty easy for me because I had worked on radios and also built some for friends and family. I explained to him about my interest in electronics and how I was always tinkering with circuits.

Khanna has been in America a lot longer than us and knew his way around. We have been doing a fair amount of driving around in his car. Besides, we didn't have a car and had not done any traveling at all. Any place we went was by foot: going to the bank or shopping for groceries. Khanna let me drive his car, and this was my first experience of driving on the wrong side of the road. I treated him to a nice Indian dinner. He really enjoyed that because he had not had Indian food for some time. Later we went downstairs to watch television.

April 17

Another long break in my routine of writing in this journal, but it is better than not writing at all. I have been very busy with college work, and it has been piling up. I have been falling behind with my studies and homework. I did what I could to try to catch up and by evening I was ready for a break. That was when Khanna came, and we played bridge. Later I made dinner, and we talked very late into the night.

I had the first test of the term in Math. It went off wonderfully, and I got an A. Yesterday I had the second test of the term in EE, and I am not sure what grade I might muster. The other topic of Engineering Graphics is going along fine though I feel I could do better. There will be a test in poetry on Thursday. I just don't know why I hate poetry. I wouldn't mind writing it occasionally, but I don't like the reading part, least of all when it is a college assignment. Anyway, I will muddle through and hope to get a passing grade.

Ranjit was called to the college office, and he asked me to go with him. Essentially he was put on probation because he was not doing well, which would explain him being down in the dumps.

April 19

Yesterday I got a wonderful surprise—an A in the last Electrical Engineering test. I couldn't have done better or been more surprised. That means I got an A in both tests so far this term. The other one was Math in which I had no difficulty gliding through the test. I wish I could keep up this tempo. I had an English test in poetry, and I hope to secure a C. The other test was in Engineering Graphics where I got a B. In EE lab I got a B in the one experiment. That is how the second term stands as of now. Let's see what the future has in store for me.

I got a letter from Kavita, and she said she was really impressed with my writing about my grandfather's passing, which really helped her. She read through it once and put it aside. Later she was going to write something similar about her grandmother's passing and was reading what I had written. That was when she noticed I had written that when I was seventeen and she just stared at the papers. She would definitely keep working at it until she had written something comparable. She wrote, "I hate you for making it so very difficult for me."

April 21

Got a letter from Daddy, and they have completed their move to Kashmir after spending one night along the way. It was a long journey, but Mom handled it fairly well, and they have settled in the new house. It is a small place, but would suffice for the summer. After that Mom would move to Chandigarh, Punjab where they would be building a house.

I have been studying poetry as part of my English class, and it has been going along fine. I'm not crazy about studying poetry, but I'm doing the best I can. Here is an example of what I was reading:

All these devious mazes of the world
I know not where they are leading me.
I try to call to the persons around
But no one here is heeding me.
This strange world in all its strangeness
Gives me no cause to call it good,
What if the rain falls or the flowers bloom
This cheers me not the way it should.
The chirping of the birds
The singing of the nightingale
Is the sign of spring,
But for me this music dies off in the gale.

I do not know the author of this poem. I really feel some days are like that, but this too shall pass, and brighter days will come.

April 24

It was not so wonderful a day in my own view because I'm displeased with myself for being so lax. I have gone a bit slack and lagging behind in studies. I must try harder to make up the deficiency caused by my own negligence, and this definitely should not be repeated. I realized there was so much work to be done, and I got through what I could and let the rest slide for later because I had no alternative. I must do better.

April 25

I have been rewarded for what I've done this quarter. I have scored an A in every course. Today I had my English test paper back, and I was shocked when I saw 'A' on it. I was expecting a C, but the fact I got an A indicates I did work for it. I was blown away when the English professor, Mr. Fox announced there was only one A in the test. It took all my will power to keep from jumping up and yelling, 'Yahoo!'

I got a letter from Daddy. Ravi was not accepted at the National Defense Academy, and they were disappointed. Ravi said he would try one more time after attending a preparatory course.

Daddy was happy to hear about my meeting Khanna from the boarding school:

"The joy and pleasure one feels when meeting an old classmate, who is also a close friend, is really beyond description because the intimacy is free from all formalities. One knows the other well, and you can talk on common matters without any hesitancy. I hope this contact with an old friend will make your stay there more enjoyable."

He was sympathetic about my complaint of not receiving replies to my letters. He understood how it is being in a faraway land and looking forward to letters from near and dear ones. He advised me not to get too frustrated and not let this point spoil my peace of mind.

May 4

Another long break since I last wrote in this journal. I was busy with a long series of tests, but that is not a good excuse for not writing. Today I had a math test, and there is no possibility of my not getting an A. I didn't have so good a luck in the field of Electrical Engineering where I missed an A by three points, which leaves me with a B. Let's see if I can make it up the next time. My weakness is my not knowing vector conversion, and I think I will have to spend a full week on that damn subject.

I finally got a letter from my pen pal, Marina. She wrote after two months and went about giving me all sorts of encouragement. It was a good letter from her, but she made no mention about being so late replying. I'm very happy to hear from her, and I wrote her a humorous letter. Let's see how she responds to this one.

May 6

We were invited to Mrs. Boriak's home for lunch. It was for foreign students only, and we had a wonderful afternoon. Food was very good, and later there were games: badminton, basketball, football, volleyball and other activities. She wanted to dance with me and just wouldn't take no for an answer. It didn't matter I couldn't dance. "Just follow my lead," was her command. I really didn't know what that meant. What could I do but make a fool of myself. It wasn't such a big deal because most of the other foreign students didn't know how to dance either. We made quite a sight—a five-foot person and a six-foot person dancing together. It must have taken some time to get the crick out of her neck. Afterward we all went for a walk, and she showed us the places of importance including the romantic ones where boys took their dates. Food was plentiful, and she gave us the leftovers to take home. I was also introduced to pie a-la mode.

I received a letter from Daddy, and he related an incident where Mom was rather broken up about my being away. Here is what he wrote:

"Last week we had friends over for dinner, and we talked about you a lot. In fact on that occasion your mom gave way to her emotions. She had to rush to the bathroom to wash her rolling tears while we were having pudding. At that moment we were all talking about the oven you had built, and she had used it to prepare the egg pudding. There was a slight pause in the conversation and a little embarrassment on the part of the guests. Then everybody realized it was a mother's heart giving way to the outwardly show. She overcame the momentary emotional feeling and was fine after that. I know off and on she feels the separation, and she sheds a few tears in her alone moments. That was the only time I saw her giving way to her feelings in the presence of others. She also felt it was not good on her part, but I suppose it was very natural, and she couldn't help it."

That was a very hard letter for me to read. I have been missing Mom also and knew she was missing me. I'm sure my being gone has been very hard for her because she has more time on her hands and feels lonely while I am buried here with minimal free time. Get up early, make breakfast, rush off to classes, make lunch, do homework, back to classes, take a short nap if time permitted, more studying, help with dinner as needed, some recreation, study more and go to sleep at one. In between there had to be time made available to socialize and catch up with correspondence. Weekends were taken up with studying, cleanup and shopping. My being in the boarding school for five years also had immunized me from being homesick because I had no Mommy or Daddy to run to for anything. We had very little spare time because we were kept busy with a fairly strict regimen, and participation in afternoon sports was mandatory. On top of that the school was six days a week.

May 16

I have not heard from Kavita for some time, and I hope she is doing okay because I'm really worried about her. I wrote to her again to lift her spirits because I fully understood her situation.

I wrote a letter to Daddy, and told him about driving we had been doing in Khanna's car. He wanted to go see friends in Akron, Ohio. It was one in the morning, and he decided to hit the road. I was not too sure about that, but he prodded us to come along. He told us we could sleep since he would be driving. We agreed and off we went, but who could sleep? We arrived there at eight, had a short visit and drove back.

I got a letter from Maldev. He wanted to know what was going on and how I was doing. He gave me information about various colleges. I had asked him about that.

Here is what I wrote to Daddy about my performance in college:

"There have been more successes for me in the studies here. In English I got a B and in Electrical Engineering an A. I bet you will not be able to guess the next subject—Math. I got an A and the top position in the class. The professor told us what the highest score was, and it turned out to be mine. All the students in this class are top performers—having a GPA of 3.5 or higher. Getting to the top of this class means more to me. You might remember I wrote to you I had gotten an A in English. I learned later that was the only A in the class, which absolutely blew my mind."

May 21

I received a letter from Kavita. It was sullen, and she said she was still down in the dumps from the double whammy of her grandma passing away and missing me. She just didn't know which way to turn. She was looking forward to rejoining the university in the fall. She thanked me for writing to her because she really enjoyed my letters and was sorry about being so lax in replying.

Just a small note about my math professor. I have been working hard to keep my grade secret when I get my test papers back. Despite my best efforts another student would peek while I carefully checked my grade. It is not always possible to stop that. On the other hand, if my grade was the highest, the math professor would announce the highest grade while looking at me. That would be the giveaway, and the others would also look at me. I'm getting rather exasperated by this. I wonder if he is trying to goad the rest of the class to do better. I remember not doing well in one test and my score of 73 confirmed it. The professor said, "I guess that was a very hard test. The highest score was 73." I was blown away.

May 23

I would like to mention an incident in today's math class. The professor was going over the differential equations. Later he gave a quiz to solve an equation. I solved it in three steps by using a different procedure than he had outlined. The professor noticed I was sitting there and came over to see if I needed help. I told him I had solved the equation, and he couldn't believe that. He looked at my solution and just shook his head because he knew it was correct. Later he showed the class his procedure to solve the equation. Then he showed them how I had solved it in a significantly shorter time.

I wrote a letter to Kavita and told her I was sorry about the delay. The term was coming to an end, and I was very busy studying for finals.

I also mentioned I might be heading to California because summer jobs in Indiana were scarce for a turbaned Indian. I was letting her know what was going on with me, and I asked her to write immediately so I would get her letter before I left. I gave her Khanna's address in case she was late in replying because I might not have an address in California for some time.

The radio has been working really well, and sometimes the reception is just the same as we used to get in India, which really lifts our spirits. It is very popular and we have quite a crowd every day. The reception is limited to about an hour and a half and then it fades out. It's fortunate we get good reception from an old junk radio I purchased for five dollars.

I purchased a '53 Oldsmobile 98 for my trip to California.

June 4

It's been a few days since I last wrote in this journal. I have to face facts that it seems to be all over between Ranjit and myself, and I'm nearing the end of my patience with him. I've been trying to avoid doing anything to upset him because he gets irritated and long-faced at the smallest things, which has pushed me to the limit. Recently he wanted to go out for a drive, but I refused because was we each had a bottle of beer. He pulled a long face, and sat down on the hood of the car. I was completely justified in not going out in that condition because he has a learner's permit and has very little experience. Still I made the mistake of agreeing to go out if he wouldn't insist on driving, and he reluctantly agreed. We got more friends aboard, and in their presence he pressured me to let him drive. I refused, and he asked me to drop him at another friend's house. I did, and he has been impossible to live with since.

My GPA last quarter was nearly 3 while his was just above 2. I won't go along with him to some so-so college just to keep him company. After summer I'll be getting out of this place, and I'm not sure I'd be glad to have him along unless he changes his ways.

June 6

Daddy was concerned about our driving around in Khanna's car:

"You have written about your long driving trips. Please be on the safe side of the speed limits. The roads may be very good, and you may be a very careful driver, but you have to take into account others who drive after drinking a lot. If you are driving rather slowly the chances of averting any mishaps are better. I don't mean one should just crawl along on good roads, but what I want to stress is your safety. The roads might be good, but the number of vehicles is much higher, and speeding is the order of the day. Remember the two major accidents that happened to Marina and her daddy." (My note: they both were in major car crashes.)

I wrote to Daddy about the second term coming to an end, and that summer job prospects in Fort Wayne being bleak. I told him to hold letters and parcels because I was not too sure where I might end up during the summer vacation. I would let him know my address as soon as I get settled. I also told him I appreciated his comments about our driving routines. I told him I would pass his thoughts on to Khanna because it was his car, and he was the driver.

June 9

Ranjit got a summer job in Chicago. He had told me some time back he would be able to get me a job there, but he just informed me he was unable to do that. Actually the message was conveyed to me by a mutual friend because he was not talking to me. I had a strong possibility of getting job through efforts of another student, but I had turned it down because of what Ranjit had said. They had hired someone else when I checked back with them. Khanna and I agreed my best bet was to go to California. I would be able to catch up with Maldev and look into transferring to a college there. We looked at the map, and decided Route 40 would be the most convenient way to go. Khanna gave me a contact in Stockton who would advise me, and I obtained a work permit from the Immigration Service.

Mrs. Boriak heard I was leaving for California, and she had us over for dinner, which was very nice of her. The main thing she emphasized was to watch going around the curves in the mountains. If the sign said 25 MPH, they meant it. I had never driven in mountains and took her advice to heart.

Chapter 3

Off to California

June 19

  I drove to California. I didn't have any time to make journal entries over the long 2,700-mile drive because the objective was to get here as fast as possible. In my letter to Daddy (below) I described the trip from Indiana to Stockton, California. The last part (California) was rather important because along the way we stopped in Stockton, Kansas. I was quite surprised when I saw the sign proclaiming Stockton off Route 40, and we had a short visit there. I'm sure we surprised a lot of people with our appearance along the way because they had never seen anything like the two Sikhs who breezed through the small towns on Highway 40.

  I had three paying passengers along for the trip. The other thing was the mile-after-mile of boring drive through the heart of the country. We slept in the car except for the first night. Most of those were short naps, because we just had to keep going. Most of the road was straight as an arrow as far as the eye could see, and I tried to beat the boredom by daydreaming about Kavita. We arrived in California and settled in a hotel in Dinuba, which is more like a dorm, and we just were renting the beds.

  I wrote a letter to Maldev letting him know I had arrived in California, and I would come see him when I had some spare time. I sent him copies of my transcripts and asked him if Fresno State College would accept me.

  The following letter to Daddy describes the long drive from Indiana to Stockton, California.

My dear Daddy,   June 19

I'm sure you must be upset with me for not writing sooner. You have every reason to be mad, but I have a good excuse for not writing, and it's not laziness. I drove a total distance of 2,710 miles, and I am now in California. For the trip I bought a 1953 Oldsmobile for one-hundred-fifteen dollars. It is in very good shape and runs beautifully. The bus fare from Indiana would have been sixty-five dollars. I brought three riders with me, and they paid thirty-five dollars each. The trip cost me seventy-two dollars, which left me with thirty-three dollars. I saved the bus fare so I am ahead ninety-eight dollars, which meant the car cost me seventeen dollars. I now have my own transportation, which is a huge advantage in California.

I know you are anxious to hear about my trip. I left Fort Wayne on the fourteenth at one in the morning. The night was pleasant, but what was not pleasant was the thought of those twenty-seven-hundred miles ahead of me. I had to do all the driving without relief because I was the only one with a license. I had a wonderful drive for the first few hours because there was no traffic, and the cities were deserted. I had one big drawback—I didn't get any sleep on the night previous to the start of the trip, or the night I started. I know you might be upset, but you don't know how things are here. It is hard going to bed when friends get together, which was especially true when I was leaving for California.

I had an agreement with myself that I would take a nap the moment I felt sleepy. The road was completely dark between towns, and after midnight the radio stations were off the air. We all worked to keep me awake, but even that was a bit of a problem because my friends were falling asleep. We finally agreed they would take turns telling me stories to keep me awake. That way they could sleep, but at least one of them had to be awake.

By dawn I had gone past the state of Indiana and I was having a wonderful drive without any hitch at all. That gave me new vigor, and I was doing better at staying awake. The landscape was pretty much constant—farmland on both sides and hardly any trees in sight. The land was absolutely flat, and the road was perfectly straight for miles on end. In the early hours I was averaging sixty, and we had food with us so could eat when we were hungry.

I started feeling really drowsy around one in the afternoon,. I pulled off the road and we slept in the car for two hours. We were off again, and at eight we called it a day after driving one thousand and three miles. It came to an average of fifty-two and a half miles per hour, which included rest stops and eating along the way. That night we spent in a hotel, and I slept like a log.

We got up at nine the next morning, and at nine-thirty we were back on the road. After going a hundred miles I smelled burning rubber, which was caused by hot gases from the defective muffler. We used milk to put the fire out because we didn't have water. We had burnt rubber and burnt milk smell to contend with for some time. Fortunately it was not that serious, and at the next service station I had a new muffler installed, which took some time. We drove through Denver, a large city, which slowed us down a lot. Around two in the morning I started feeling drowsy. I pulled off to the side of the road, and we all slept in the car. That day we did six hundred miles. We were back on the road at seven, and that day I did another seven hundred miles. On the fourth day at eleven in the morning we reached Stockton, California, and we lodged temporarily at the Sikh Temple.

The journey as a whole was quite tiring but very good. The car handled the trip with commanding ease, and we didn't have any major breakdown. Apart from the muffler trouble, there was another episode when the car refused to move. Fortunately there was a repair shop only a hundred yards away, and I was able to get it fixed for less than a dollar. The mechanic replaced a small bolt on the fuel pump that had fallen off.

I also had a tire blow out, and the car veered sharply. I corrected immediately and brought it to a safe stop. I applied the brakes very sparingly, and let the car slow down on its own. The left front tire had blown—the most dangerous one. I was able to avoid a major mishap without any fuss. We changed the wheel and were off again. The blown tire had a bad effect on the others, and I told them all to pipe down. At the next town I had the tire replaced.

The drive was a wonderful experience for me. I encountered all sorts of conditions and came through without any problems. There were stretches of level plains where the road was visible for miles, and the land was flat as it could be. There was a mountain range where I couldn't go more than twenty miles an hour.

Speed limits varied from 50 to no limit at all. That's right—there was no speed limit in the state of Nevada. The roads were divided with double lanes for each side of traffic. The maximum speed I drove was 105, which was not full throttle, and I didn't push it any further. It was too tempting because the road was straight and visible for miles on end. Also the road was divided, and there was no other car within a couple of miles. I was also goaded by my friends who wanted to see the car go one hundred. I know you don't feel very good after your sermon about keeping on the safe side of the speed limit. One thing I can assure you is I did keep on the safe side. (Difficult to keep on the safe side of the speed limit when there is no speed limit at all.) I'm not very sure how to convince you. If I went at high speeds, it was after making sure it was safe. That is the reason I didn't have any major mishaps during the 2,710 miles I drove in four days.

Soon after my arrival here I got a temporary job picking peaches and plums, and had high hopes of getting a permanent one soon. Even if I didn't get one, I had transportation and could move about while looking for a job. I wasn't dependent on others to take me around. In that short time I was earning ten dollars a day. I was not satisfied and was on the lookout for a better paying job. A couple of days later I found a steady job. I was making fifteen dollars daily, but was still not happy, but I stuck to it to get to know the job. The work was tough, and there was a lot to do. The first few days were very hard, and the nights were spent sleeping like a log. Soon everything changed, and I could do hard work more easily.

Looking forward to hearing from you soon.

Yours affectionately,

Rajinder

June 20

I got an apartment for the summer and passed the address to Daddy. I wrote to Kavita and included a copy of the letter I wrote to Dad about my trip across the country. I also related to her all the hard work I had to do to keep things moving along, which should give her a good idea how it was for me. I didn't have much else to add because I had just arrived in California.

Busy, busy days and I was working hard to keep my head above water. Looking for a job in the various fruit packing houses was a huge challenge. Being turned down at every place I asked was very disheartening. There was never a question about my qualifications. They would just look at me, and summarily say there was no opening. In the meantime I continued picking peaches, plums and the like in 105 degree weather. That was very hard work—going up and down the ladder, moving the ladder and moving on. It took a few days, and my body had to adjust to the new rigors of life.

July 9

I got a letter from Kavita, and she was happy to hear from me after a relatively long break. She was absolutely blown away when she read about my trip across the country. She asked, "Why didn't you fly there? Ha ha!" She also wrote:

"I'm not happy you didn't tell me how far California was. Neither am I happy that you didn't sleep the night before your trip or the night of your trip. On top of that you were driving like a madman. Do you have a secret death wish? I'm relieved you arrived there safely despite your best efforts to the contrary!"

That was the first time she was upset with me, and I didn't blame her because I deserved it. A twenty-year old doesn't think things through and she put a whole new light on my trip. I was rather reckless and should have known better. Driving at over a hundred miles an hour was not such a good idea either.

July 15

Daddy replied to my letter, and he was rather pleased with what I had to say about the car. I have included that here in its entirety:

My dear Rajinder,

We are very much relieved to hear you are keeping fit. We congratulate you about your new possession, and your account of the long journey is very thrilling. I wonder how a used car costing so little could run such long distances with so few breakdowns. I'm very confident about your driving practice, and I'm sure you put safety before anything else. The only thing I want to emphasize is that accidents do take place and the faster the vehicle speed at the time of the accident, more the damage.

I was relieved to hear you are okay after the tire burst, and you had everything under control. Such things can happen when one is slightly off guard, and then the result can be very serious. I feel speeds of sixty to seventy are not excessive on really good roads, and faster than that it is not safe. I know you will figure I don't know the conditions in that country. You may be correct in these assumptions, but may I remind you about what happened to your pen pal, Marina and her father. We are apt to consider somebody else making a mistake, and thereby can have an accident but not ourselves. So always bear in mind your speed should be such that you are in control of the vehicle without damage at the time of any accidental breakdown. No more sermon, and I hope you will take this in the spirit it is given.

Buying the car was a wise decision, and I fully appreciate the advantage of owning one's own transport. It will help you in saving a lot of precious time, which you can utilize doing some part-time jobs. Your mom is very happy you have your own transport and was slightly worried when I read to her the speeds at which you were driving. I have explained to her the road conditions, and she felt quite relieved after that.

Yours affectionately,
Daddy

July 17

Daddy wondered about my choice of Fresno State College where I would get a degree in two years. He figured it was rather a short time and wanted to know if the college was properly accredited. He said the decision was mine, and he was only expressing his concern. He also asked if I needed to go back to Indiana for my transcripts or any luggage I might have left behind. He was quite concerned about my driving at excessive speeds, and I appreciated that. I wondered if I should have told him everything. I have decided to share it all with him, and I wanted to continue doing that. He was very pleased with the purchase of the car and said it was a good idea. He said they were in the process of packing for Mom's move back to Punjab. Ravi was unavailable again because he was checking out universities for his fall enrollment.

I got a letter from Maldev, and he was looking forward to seeing me. He sent me an application for transferring to Fresno State College, and I shouldn't have any problem getting accepted. He asked me to let him know when I would be coming so he could arrange to go to the college with me. (I didn't have a telephone because I couldn't afford it.)

I managed to adjust to the tough going in the Central Valley, California. I wasn't very strong because I was not used to physical labor. The first job I got here was picking fruit, which was a rough start. It involved climbing the ladder, picking the fruit, coming down and moving the ladder to the next tree. Seemed like I was not working fast enough, and on the third day I was fired. I went looking for other work and found a job pulling suckers off the grapevines. They grew at the very bottom of the vine and come off easily. Still, it is tough bending down, pulling the suckers off, standing up and walking to the next vine. My back got quite a workout, and that night was very uncomfortable. There is no chance of waiting for it to adjust because I had to go back the following day and continue on.

I received the results from Fort Wayne, Indiana for my second term. I have improved my grade point average to 3.58 from 2.94 previous term, and I passed them on to Daddy.

July 18

I wrote to Kavita and thanked her for her comment about my flying to California. In other words, I should have bought an airline ticket to California instead of buying a car! One hundred and fifteen dollars would have been more than enough for the fare! (Ha ha!). Told her I loved her sense of humor and would consult with her the next time I went on a trip of that magnitude.

I also wrote,

"I apologize about my recklessness, and I won't be doing stupid things like that anymore, or drive even close to a hundred miles an hour. I guess thinking carefully was not my forte at the time because I was tempted by the wide-open road, no traffic and no speed limit. I was also being goaded by my friends to go for it because they wanted to see the car do a hundred! I was in the camp of the army officer who gave this command, 'Ready, fire, aim!' Sure fit my mental aptitude at the time.

"It also goes along the line of my being the adventurous type. If that wasn't the case then I wouldn't have left India where I would have stayed safe and secure with Mom and Daddy! If that had been the case then I wouldn't have been on that ship for you to lasso!

"I know the following statement might confuse you. Luckily you are also the adventurous type. If you weren't you wouldn't have come charging to my side of the ship—twice! You would have stayed safe and secure with your mom and daddy, and I wouldn't have been able to come there to lasso you!

"In other words, we're both rather unconventional and move to a different drumbeat, and in my opinion that is what makes us special. Feel free to disagree with me!"

I didn't tell her I wouldn't be driving that fast in California because the speed limit was 65 MPH as opposed to no limit in Nevada.

July 20

I went to San Jose to meet Sib, another classmate from the boarding school, and he was really surprised to see me. He suggested we go to Santa Cruz for a leisurely day, but was rather skeptical about my car making it over the hill considering what I had paid for it. On the way there I noticed a few cars on the side of the road with steaming radiators, but my car performed flawlessly. I fully expected that because it had conquered the Rockies whereas this was just a hillock in comparison. We had a great time visiting the beach, and seeing all those girls in their swimsuits. I had never been at a beach because I lived several hundred miles from the ocean. Late in the afternoon I dropped him back at his place, and got back home late.

July 22

Daddy asked about the horsepower of my car. My friends told me it was 250, and I passed that on to him.

I went to Fresno to meet Maldev. It was very nice seeing him again, and we had quite a reunion. We drove to the college, and I applied for admission. The clerk looked over my transcripts and told me there shouldn't be any problem. He had me sign forms so he could order the paperwork from Indiana. I would be receiving credit for my B.S. degree from India and thirty six units from Indiana.

Maldev and I spent the rest of the day checking out apartments. We wouldn't be living together because he already had a roommate, Jo. They had been together for a couple of years, and he introduced us. Jo said he enjoyed meeting me, and Maldev had talked about me quite a lot. Later in the afternoon I drove back to Dinuba and talked to the three students who came with me from Fort Wayne. They were fully expecting me to stay in California, and I made it final. I told them I would be with them through the summer and then drop them off at the bus depot for their trip back to Indiana.

July 26

Daddy's response to my second term results was wonderful:

"Yesterday I received your letter enclosing the transcript from last term. I was really overwhelmed to hear about your achievement and congratulate you heartily for the same. What else can a father expect from his son? You've found your capabilities, and I'm sure you will make the best use of your talents that so far had been lying dormant. Your mother is also proud of your success."

July 30

Job hunting has been a huge problem, and finding an apartment was equally challenging. In a letter to Daddy I alluded to some of these problems I have been running into. Here is part of what I wrote to him about some of what I was talking about:

"In this desolate place your letters are the only thing that keeps my spirits up. The word desolate in the above sentence might surprise you. It's not desolate in the literal sense but in another sense. That is not just my opinion, but all the multitudes of other foreigners. They learn this first hand and become painfully aware of public opinion in this country. I'll write you a detailed letter on this subject sometime later because I want you to know it all."

I thanked him for his congratulatory message about the results from the last term, and now I could really feel I'd earned it. The whole responsibility was on my shoulders, and I had learned so much in those few months.

I wrote to him about the hood on the car flying open. I was unhurt, but the car's windshield needed to be replaced.

August 14

Got a letter from Kavita, and she was relieved to hear I wouldn't be driving at breakneck speeds anymore. She accepted my explanation about my rationale at the time, and said she realized guys goad each other into doing stupid things. She had seen and heard about those types of things from her friends. She wrote:

"A friend lost her brother while performing a bicycle jump. He was not keen on doing that, but his friends pushed and goaded him. The jump was not very high, but he fell when he landed sideways and his head hit a rock. Another friend had just performed that jump and had landed safely. I know it is not a good comparison, but that is what flashed in my mind when I read your account. I'm sure you don't have that much driving experience, but you handled the situations well. My mind jumped to that bike accident, and I was really shaken up. I'm sorry about making such a big deal out of it, and thank you for being so understanding.

"Your comment about being adventurous type really hit me hard, and I just sat there staring into space. That was a very scary thought—you not being on that ship. I can't imagine what that voyage and the last few months would have been like without you. That thought sent chills up and down my spine, and you put a whole new light on the subject. I sat there reliving our time together on the ship. Then I thought about you not being there. The only thing I could think of was my aimlessly wandering the hallways and the main deck because that is what I did on my previous two voyages. The time would have dragged on and on, which brought tears to my eyes and slowly I pulled myself out of that reverie."

August 18

Daddy was getting quite concerned about what I thought were trivial things. I was getting rather bugged about his responses and wrote to him about that in the following letter:

"Going through your letters I have a strange feeling of amusement and slight annoyance. I'm really amused at the way you write things, and how you give me a piece of your mind in the guise of advice. I'm slightly annoyed by the way you feel upset by the minor things that go on here. You see I'm making you my wholehearted partner to all my experiences here. I want to share everything with you, and I'm not apt to keep things from you. I know people here who have had most disastrous accidents. One person broke his leg and had a severe injury to his back, but he kept quiet and never wrote a word about it to his parents. I wonder if you want me to be like that. I want to share everything with me—my joys, my moments of anxiety and my moments of supreme pride.

"On the other hand you have not been like a lot of other Indian fathers. I've heard other students tell me about all the restrictions imposed upon them. They had to swear they wouldn't do this or that, but you did nothing of the sort. Apart from some minor things, you did not stress much of anything. You left it all entirely up to me—how I should behave and how I should act.

"I'm also not being like the others who keep everything from their parents. I have avoided that because I want to share everything with you, for it is something new. I don't want to keep this all to myself—what is the use of that? You were happy to hear my results of the last term as I wanted you to be. On the other hand, I wanted you to be proud about how I handled the tire blowout, but you were really concerned. I know it. I expected you to be proud of my ability to stay cool, calm and composed in the biggest of the emergencies as demonstrated by the last two incidents.

"Just three days before I left Indiana a friend described an accident he had witnessed. The front tire burst, the car flipped over five times, and four women in that car died. That accident was on my mind, but I didn't panic. The other driver was going only sixty, and I was traveling eighty-five at the time of the blowout. I didn't tell you about the first accident because I knew you would be very concerned. Now I want you to know about it so you can compare the two blowouts. One was at a lower speed, which resulted in four deaths. The other occurred at a higher speed where I had the car under control a fraction of a second after the blowout.

"Speed does count in these things, but it is the ability of the driver, and his presence of mind is the deciding factor between little or no damage and a fatal accident. I had read about another accident caused by the hood popping open. The car veered to the left and smashed head-on into a truck. The driver of the car was killed instantly while the truck driver suffered severe injuries. Why didn't that happen to me? That's because I didn't panic at the wrong time.

"Regarding the choice of Fresno State College, there were various factors influencing my decision. It is a state college—just the same as Punjab University where I obtained my B.S. degree.

"I've brought my luggage with me, and I have no need to go back to Indiana. I haven't added much to my belongings since I arrived here. I have purchased a pair of work shoes because I was ruining the good ones, and I have also bought a pair of work pants."

Daddy's response to my above letter was wonderful. Here is an excerpt: (Full letter in Appendix.)

"I must say I've really liked your frank and straightforward letters, and I've read most of those to my friends. They have admired the way you have been getting through your day-to-day life in America. You can't expect a father who has no bent of mind toward car races to tell his son, 'Well done boy, keep it up and let us see how you fare in a blowout at a greater speed.' I do have love and affection that keeps goading me to write to you to be careful and go slow. This can only come from parents and from nobody else.

"I'm not trying to restrict your movements. You can do what you want and go where you want—just go a bit slower. As for my confidence in your presence of mind and your capabilities, I had no doubt earlier and have none now. This in fact is the reason I didn't fill your ears with so much advice when you left for your studies. You must also have seen by now I am a man of few words, and I only say those things that must be said. Just think if nobody shows any anxiety about one's welfare, what does one claim in this life? When you get married there will be another partner who will be able to show anxiety. Until then it is only mother and father who will bother about you and keep on bothering about you. Don't for a moment think I didn't appreciate your coolness of mind just because I didn't say, 'Well done, boy'. Something prevented me from saying that aloud, and that something is love and affection.

"I'll keep on expecting these frank letters from you. Even if I seem scared after hearing any of your incidents, don't bother about it. A piece of advice from parents or well wishers can always be taken or ignored based on the merits of each individual case. If you really want us to stop offering any kind of advice, we will do so. We can't be right in all cases, and we are not aware of the conditions over there. Still something in us compels up to tell our son to be careful. I'm sure that is the natural consequence of hearing about some incident that could have resulted in greater damage and injury.

"Your explanation for the change of college is very sound. I didn't know there are colleges that give credit for a B. S. degree from India. I really fail to understand why colleges in India don't allow such concessions, which is beyond me. There is such a vast contrast in the systems of education. Then again, America is a land of contrasts."

Daddy put out the fire I had started with my previous letter by being really over the top. Any other Indian dad wouldn't have responded as he did. I will have to tell him I appreciated his response.

August 20

I finally found a job for the summer at a fruit packinghouse. The foreman, Mr. Nikos took a chance on me. He was from Greece and was aware of challenges I was facing. Some of the workers were students from Fresno State College, and they were excited about my being there. They were mostly senior to me and ready to graduate. They all volunteered to help me in any way they could. After all I had been through it was rather nice to get this support from those youngsters. At lunch breaks we would sit together and talk about the college. They had a lot of questions about my background.

Also many of my co-workers were Mexican, and it was interesting interacting with them. One of them, Oscar was in a senior position, and I talked to him at every opportunity. He was fascinated about my being a foreign student who already had a college degree. He was very helpful and gave me pointers about the various jobs. Oscar was very aware of the discrimination I had been running into. I told him about the problem I was having finding an apartment. He pointed me to places for me to try, and I managed to find the apartment for the summer with his help.

I stopped by the college, and decided on my courses with the help of Maldev. He was a senior and had no problem getting courses he wanted. Later we went apartments hunting. I rented an apartment with another Indian student who was a new arrival. Later I had to rush back to Dinuba to a job I had lined up for the afternoon.

I wrote to Daddy about our exchange of letters. His recent response was wonderful and really got to me. Here is my letter to him:

My Dear Daddy,   September 14

Your last letter was wonderful—something I'll cherish all my life. It's not that I was in any way scared about your response. I'm really proud of you and everything you stand for. I don't know how I had lost my sense of reasoning by not seeing all the points you raised. You are very right in doing the things your way. So what if I fly off the handle now and then? I feel this is good for the emotions, and anger suppressed tends to be destructive. The only bad thing is you were the unintended target of some of that.

You did throw me off by your previous letter, and I'm not ashamed to admit it. In this strange country I can only look to you for affection and consideration. Otherwise who can I turn to during those moments? Sometimes I do feel lonely, and I really miss you all in some of my depressive moments. You see I'm taking it the hard way, and I know these days I will remember all my life. The last nine months will be etched in my memory like a photograph.

Yours affectionately,
Rajinder

September 16:

I received a letter from Kavita. She sounded much better after joining the university, although it was a challenge getting back into the swing of things. She was happy because the university helped to focus her mind. She met interesting girls and made new friends. She told me not to worry about her because she'll be doing fine. She was not happy about my not having a telephone. That was a wonderful letter as compared to earlier letters that were rather sullen, and I was happy to see the change.

Work is progressing, and I am better able to handle the physical part work. It's a lot of hard work, which is causing some thickening under my nails and wonder if this would be permanent. Other than that there seem to be no other physical problems.

Daddy was happy about my comments:

"I never thought I was annoyed with your letter of the eighteenth of August, and I rather liked your frank expression of views. Anyway, my reply to that must be already in your hands, and I don't want to delve into that subject anymore. The only thing I want to say is keep on confiding in us your feelings of joy and excitement, including any worries. Let us all share your life in America. We might be showing little concern about certain things, which is a genuine wish about your well-being, but don't bother about that, and let's continue sharing each other's views."

<u>September 26</u>

  I arrived in California on June the eighteenth after finishing the spring term in Indiana. I managed to find a job, but was fired after three days because I was not working fast enough. After a lot of hunting I landed a job in a fruit packinghouse that I kept for the summer. That closed at the end of the season, and I was on the road again. I did some odd fruit picking, and tree pruning jobs. That brought summer vacation to a close, and I joined Fresno State College. Sounds simple, doesn't it? The whole story of my summer vacation condensed in a short paragraph.

  It hadn't been easy because I arrived at the college with hardly enough money in my pocket to keep me going. I was having a taste of life the hard way. My only source of income was ten to twenty dollars I earned over the weekend, but expenses were high, and money didn't last very long. Mr. Miyamoto of the Farm Labor Office was very helpful to me. He knew my schedule of needing jobs over the weekend, and invariably had something lined up for me for at least one day. One incident really brought home the discrimination problem. He sent me on a job and the farmer told me he didn't need me. I figured he might have hired someone else and went back to the Farm Labor Office. Mr. Miyamoto wanted to know why I was not at the job, and I explained what happened. He called the farmer and wanted to know why he didn't put me to work. He got quite angry at him and hung up. He realized why I was not hired, and told me that farmer's requests for workers would have lowest priority! I was grateful Mr. Miyamoto was looking out for me.

  I wrote a letter to Kavita and told her I was glad she was concentrating on her studies. She has been complaining about my not having a telephone. That was because I couldn't afford one. I also missed talking with her and would enjoy hearing her lovely voice. I had been working very hard during the summer. Unfortunately, the car needed attention, and I had to spend a lot of money to keep it going. College had started, and I was getting settled in the new town. Also gave her a rundown of the college and Fresno where life would be so much nicer without snow. Told her I really enjoyed her letters and was anxiously looking forward to them.

Chapter 4

Trial by Fire

October 1:

I just got back from Reedly, a town twenty-six miles from Fresno, and it was a day of grueling work. I earned ten dollars and collected money due me from an earlier account. The expenses of the car also came up. It was almost a losing battle because expenses keep piling up, and the money went out faster than it came in.

Things were just dragging along. Apart from studies, there was the big problem of money. I was broke most of the time, and there was no running away from that fact. My sole dependence was on the money I earned over the weekend, and that would disappear in a hurry. The summer was not too good because money I earned was mostly used for car repairs. Then there was the minor accident when the hood of the car flew open and broke the windshield. That cost me fifty dollars. Next I needed a set of tires, which cost ninety dollars. Then the battery went dead and a new one cost twenty dollars. Other expenses had been piling up. I had almost nothing left after paying college fees and other expenses. Every weekend I went looking for a job, and the luck always favored me.

October 7

This was another one of the tough weekends, and I was almost ready to drop off to sleep right here on the typewriter. Yesterday I started a job of picking grapes at ten in the morning. I worked until five, and I had another job lined up at six at a fruit-packing shed. I hand-trucked the grapes from the receiving station to the packing station. I was handling the job of two men, and I put in four more hours there. Firstly, the job of picking grapes was tough on my back, and I was ready to collapse. Secondly, the packing shed job was heavy on my arms and legs. The job involved a lot of walking and pushing heavy boxes. For the night I found a parking place and slept in the car because a motel would have cost half my day's wages.

I didn't even have a blanket because I hadn't been able to afford one. In Indiana I was provided with a furnished apartment and didn't want for anything. Here I didn't have a fully furnished apartment, and I was having a rather tough time getting along. I was hoping my overcoat would get me through this night, but the car got very cold. By the time I woke I was definitely chilled. In the morning I started the car, and the heater warmed me.

I was picking grapes, and my hands almost froze from heavy dew and cold. I warmed them on the exhaust of the tractor a number of times. I didn't get enough rest during the night due to the cramped condition in the car, and my legs were aching. All these factors made me extremely slow, and I wondered if the boss would be upset. He showed up at ten, and I was ready to quit because hardly any grapes were picked. I told him the cold was slowing me down, and I asked him if he wanted me to quit. He smiled and told me not to worry because I would be doing better as the day warmed up. He joined me picking grapes for about an hour. I was feeling better by that time, but after lunch it was another tough going. My picking was better, but my condition was miserable. I could hardly do the necessary squatting and standing as needed. By the end of the day my legs were ready to cave in.

This went on day-after-day as the expenses would come up and money would disappear in a hurry. The big rush was for the rent due on the eighteenth, and I was able to pay it. I had never done this kind of physical work in my life. This is brand new and quite challenging for me. I just had to keep going, and my body adjusted.

October 15

Got a letter from Kavita. She sounded better and was enjoying her studies at the university. She has taken three village girls under her wing and helping them adjust to city life. They are very appreciative and couldn't thank her enough. She was missing me and again wanted to know when I was getting a telephone.

The following is a letter to Daddy, which lays out all I had gone through during my nine and a half months in this country. It covers the discrimination I had suffered and tough time I had all the way around.

My dear Daddy,   October 18

Sorry I'm late in replying to your last letter because I have been exceedingly busy since college started, although not been as busy as I was during summer vacation.

I am really happy to hear Brother has been accepted at the National Defense Academy, and I've written him a letter of congratulations. He will be a commissioned officer by the time I return, and I'm rather envious. Military service was not slated for me. I tried two times and was not accepted. Whether it was for good or not, I cannot say.

The car is fine, but keeps making demands for repairs. During vacation it needed new tires, a battery, a generator and a spare tire. It is easy to say I have a car, but it is damnably hard to keep it on the road. The only thing is I cannot do without it, and its reliance is unquestionable.

Now I would like to elaborate on some of the things I had mentioned in my previous letters. I know you are interested because you have asked about them. Once again I want to ask you not to panic or get mad when you hear everything because I have my own ways of dealing with these situations.

You asked me about my finances. I will give it to you, but give me your assurance you will not panic. My financial situation is nil. Yes, that is true, and you asked for it. If you have any confidence in my abilities, you should know I'll be fine. At the present moment I have twenty-two dollars in my pocket and twenty dollars in the bank. I'm not worried a bit because on the weekend I will earn another fifteen to twenty dollars, and that will tide me over for the week. I will not hesitate to ask for your help if I'm really hard up because I have no other place to turn, but for minor things I won't trouble you.

I had mentioned the problems I was having with my roommate, Ranjit. He was the most difficult person to get along with, and from him I've learned quite a few lessons. The first one is never getting too familiar with anyone here. I wrote to you earlier about some of his really strange notions, and I'm ashamed to admit I followed some of them. He would get mad at me over something minor and give me the silent treatment. On the most minor jokes he would turn up his nose and wouldn't answer a direct question. Matters came to a head after I bought the car. I knew that might happen, and I had spoken to Khanna about it because I had faith in his judgment. He understood my point, and he said he'd try to have the matters straightened out with Ranjit. I told Khanna things were not good between us, and the car would form an insurmountable barrier. Ranjit had a learner's permit, and I had a driver's license. He was keen on driving the car, and he either cut too short on turns or swung wide. You might remember I was also like that in the beginning. We were invited to the house of an American, and I handed him the wheel. I noticed their driveway was very narrow, and a car could barely pass. I asked Ranjit to let me take the car in because I didn't want the flowerbeds trampled. After that he didn't speak a kind word to me. He argued with Khanna if he was able to handle the car along the road then why not along that driveway? I tried to speak to him a few times, but he didn't respond, and in utter frustration I gave up.

One evening Ranjit wanted to go for a drive, but I objected saying it was not proper to drive after drinking beer. He didn't like that and sat on the hood of the car with a long face. I made the mistake of agreeing to go out only if he would not insist on driving, and he reluctantly agreed. We stopped by friends' house to see if they wanted to go with us. We had the car loaded, and in their presence he insisted he be allowed to drive. I flatly refused, and he asked me to drop him at a friend's house. I did, and that was that. I had promised to drop Ranjit at his job in Chicago on my way to California, and I asked him if he wanted me to do that. He replied curtly, "No, thank you!" I turned to Khanna for help, and it was with his effort we finally parted on speaking terms.

I am also ashamed to admit I followed some of his advice. He didn't want his parents to know what was going on here. This is what I wrote to you in my letter of August the eighteenth:

"On the other hand I'm also not being like the others who keep everything from their parents. Their letters home are shrouded with lies and other nonsense."

He didn't want me to tell you about the typewriter I bought. He cited the example of his not telling his parents about the iron and radio he had purchased. I didn't listen to him and wrote you about the typewriter. He brought up the same point when I purchased the car. I am ashamed to say I didn't write to you about the car. I was going to, but he told me it would be better to tell you after a few months. I know it wasn't good not telling you the truth, but I was led to believe it was best to keep silent. I'm sorry I followed his advice. Also he had promised he would get me a job where he would be working during the summer. I missed a chance to get a job in Indiana because I thought it would be in our best interest to stay together to face the odds against us. I was a fool to agree and missed that job in Indiana. It was late in the quarter before he told me about it. Actually a friend relayed that information because he was not talking to me at the time. I packed my car and came to California, and I don't regret anything at all. I wrote to Khanna to inquire if he had heard anything from Ranjit. He wrote back he had not.

There are several lessons I won't forget, and the most important one is not to get too involved with anyone here because no one has any right over me. Ranjit acted as if he had a right over me and everything I owned. He used to drive my car with my full permission, but now I don't allow anyone to touch its steering wheel. That is the way things are here—you give an inch and the other fellow takes a mile. I know it is futile to make sacrifices for anyone. I only gained a harder job with lower pay instead of the one in Indiana. I have no regrets because it is water under the bridge. The best thing is to concentrate on the present and move on. I tried my best to get along with Ranjit. So with 'Best of luck, and take care of yourself,' we parted at least on speaking terms because of the efforts of Khanna.

In Khanna I had a very good friend. He had been in this country longer than us and had better knowledge of everything. It is true we ran around a lot, but the things I learned from him will prove invaluable. One thing he couldn't get me to do was drink Scotch Whiskey. He tried a number of times saying it was something I would have to do. I do drink beer, and I've found this to be a wonderful drink when kept within limits. I don't normally drink a full bottle. The beer bottle here is about half the size of the bottle in India.

Now I come to the topic of the more important consequence to me. It is about the treatment we receive from the local people. You might be surprised to hear they hate foreigners. That is not just my opinion, but also the general observation of foreign students and other foreigners. It is not easy living here with hatred continually present around you because you sense it in the air and feel it in the eyes of the person looking at you. You don't have to have a degree in psychology to know it's happening, nor do you have to be telepathic to sense it. You know it as plainly as if this is being shouted at you from a platform.

Interesting how we do not take heed when others try to warn us. We have our preconceived notions, and anything deviating from those just falls on deaf ears. Here is an excerpt from my journal dated March third this year:

"We went to visit Jogi, an Indian student who had been here for three quarters. The conversation we had with him was not encouraging at all. Seems to me these old-timers try pretty hard to discourage the newcomers who are trying to get their bearings. I do feel they ought to put an end to this. The main theme of what he was warning us about was all the discrimination he had suffered. We really didn't understand what he was talking about because we had experienced none of that."

Now I know first-hand what he was talking about, and it has hit me like a ton of bricks. In Indiana I was primarily in the college environment and had not gone out into the real world, but here in the Central Valley, California the real world has come at me full force. Foreigners are like ghosts to Americans. I know you might be surprised to hear that, but truth is always stranger than fiction. I had excelled in my studies in Indiana. An American's grade point average probably would have been 4.0 if he had performed at my level. Americans cannot imagine a foreigner out-classing them. I was good in math and was at the top of the class. I used to keep my grades secret, but that was not always possible, for someone would peek as I looked inside. The word would spread once again I had the highest score. On the last test I scored a B, and the student who scored the highest must have been really excited about beating me.

Considering all this I am not surprised Sikhs remove their turban and shave their beards in an effort to be less conspicuous. I know it is a big drawback for me, and I can't get a good job as long as I am wearing this turban. I also know how my back aches from working in the fields, and the first thing I can think of is sleeping after a shower. I distinctly remember how I was sneered at when I was looking for a job in the Central Valley in California. I inquired at a dozen places and asked if there was an opening, but I was turned away at every place. This was in Reedly, Dinuba and other towns in the vicinity. The one place I got a job was due to the sympathy of Nikos, a Greek foreman who was once a foreign student himself, and was aware of the difficulties facing me. How would you feel if you were rejected numerous times over the course of a few days? It is a nasty dejection getting the same smirk, as if to say, 'Go home kid. What are you doing here in America?' Was there not a single job opening out of the dozen places I visited? It's not a good feeling experiencing such prejudice, but I do have the stamina to fight on.

During the same time I had the same problem looking for an apartment. I was greeted with the same 'Sorry, the apartment has just been rented.' The 'For Rent' sign was still there, but they said the sign remained there all year—whether the apartment was rented or not. I faced all that so many times and finally found a small two-room unit with the help of a Mexican co-worker. I gave my friends the use of the double bed, and I slept on the floor. The other room was a kitchen, dining, living and entertainment room—all crammed together. They were small rooms, and it was not easy to move about briskly while getting dressed, but what can you do? You have to be content with whatever is available to you.

I know it is not a very heartening situation to live in, and I also know you will not feel good after reading this. It won't do you any good for you to worry—just let me handle it. You have my word I will watch my step, and I won't make any hasty or nasty moves. The situation is bad, but it isn't hopeless. For heaven's sake, please don't tell Mom because it's no use worrying her. You asked me to keep you informed about everything, and that's what I'm doing. I know you will worry, but will that change anything? I'm asking you to leave this up to me, and please don't spread the word because no one will believe you.

Finally I want to attribute some of my perseverance to what I read on your desk in Poona in 1952: "There is no task that will not yield to regular, patient and persistent effort." I'm very sure it didn't have any significant impact on me then because I was barely ten, and had been studying English for just a couple of years, but I'm glad it came to mind here during the tough times I've been facing. That gave me the push in the right direction.

You must have had enough of this marathon letter. It has taken me four days to write it, and I hope you have gotten the gist of what is going on. Just leave everything to me.

Do reply soon. I will be expecting your letter at the earliest.

Yours affectionately,
Rajinder

October 24

This is one of those bad days because I've had this nasty cold for the last two days, and I might not get back to my original health because of the lack of care. In India I could be assured of care from Mom. I might not be able to work this weekend. I am a bit low financially, and it is a crisis hitting me. I hope everything will be all right. It is a very disheartening feeling being here all alone without help or support from anyone. Any reply to my letter home will be two to three weeks away.

The other day I wrote a very long letter to Daddy in which I filled him in about conditions here. I gave him the inside story of the whole situation and how things are going. I don't know if I did the right thing, but I feel better getting it off my chest.

October 25

I went to the employment office and was told there were no openings. They promised to let me know if anything turned up. Jobs are scarce, and the majority of jobs require experience—something I lack. The only experience I have is the three months at the fruit-packing shed. That is in addition to the disadvantage of my turban and beard. I just don't know what to do.

It seems I'm becoming more dejected all the time, and I don't know how this will settle in. Nothing seems to matter anymore, and I'm getting in the mood of, 'So what! Let everything go to hell.' I don't like it, but also I can't help it. There are so many things I don't like, but they still happen. We don't always get what we want, and I don't think I am any exception. I can only hope things get better—seems like that is all I have left.

October 26

My friend and I went to San Francisco to get a tape recorder and recorded Indian music. Traffic was light until we got to San Francisco. Problems arose when we entered the Skyway that had three very narrow lanes and traffic was bumper-to-bumper. It was a typical example of persons being carried along in the big stream of life. More than once I was pushed in the wrong direction because I couldn't change lanes in time. I was happy when we finally reached our destination and got the tape recorder, but we were disappointed because there were only two reels of poorly recorded tape. It was about half past four in the morning by the time we got to bed. In all we covered four hundred miles in a total of fourteen hours, and the car did sixteen miles per gallon.

October 27

It has been a while since I heard from Kavita. She should have replied to my last letter by now, but she might be busy with studies. She has been out of the university and might be having problems readjusting.

I have been thinking about her, and I came to quite a realization. I have lived in a make-believe world that this would all work out in the end. We would see each other again and pick up where we left off in Genoa, because anything this special couldn't just end. I was hoping her father would have to come to America on another business trip, and she would be with him. Somehow we would manage to be with each other. This was wishful thinking and not grounded in reality. Even if we had met in Indiana, it would have been a difficult long distance romance. She couldn't stay in America because I couldn't sponsor her. I was barely able to take care of myself and had no way to show I could support her. Also Indian morés dictated we had to be married for her to stay with me. I have to face reality and continue on. She is mature beyond her years, and I desperately need this diversion for my own sake—wanting more than just the correspondence with Mom and Daddy. I am lonely and need her to fill the void. We have been going on one unshakable premise—our getting back together.

October 30

The owner of the nearby gas station was a friendly type, and I would stop there to chat with him. He introduced me to other Americans, and it was interesting meeting them. The following is an account of a talk with one of them named George. I was not sure if he was telling me the truth, or was he just telling me stuff to see how far out he could be before

I said I didn't believe a word of it. My being very naïve didn't help, because I was inclined to believe he was telling the truth. We talked for about two hours. It was a getting acquainted meeting, and we asked a lot of questions of each other.

From my point of view his attitude was rather strange. I was interested in talking to him as a typical American young man because I wanted to know about his way of thinking and his attitude. We didn't go into politics, and we didn't talk about what was going on in the world. I was only interested in knowing what he thought about me and other foreigners. He told me he was a very religious man, but I found that hard to believe because his actions didn't fit along those lines.

George seemed to be a perfect loafer who didn't seem to care a bit about his wife. He wouldn't give a second thought to going out with other women and having a wonderful time—even having sex. I wonder if that is what an average American man did. His basic argument was he gets tired of going to bed with the same woman night-after-night, and he was only looking for some change and fun. Prostitutes and wayward women were his major point of interest. He didn't care if his wife did the same behind his back, nor would he be concerned if she went with a hundred other men or had sex with any or all of them. That was quite something and had me wondering if he was really like that or telling me all that stuff just for the fun of it. I don't know.

He was commenting about my English and snickering at my pronunciations. I tried to explain to him I was speaking British/Indian English, which got him snickering more, and he was wondering why they couldn't get it right. I looked at him with amusement, which confused him. I told him as far as I was concerned those were the correct pronunciations. That made him laugh, and I had an internal laugh. I asked him what language was spoken in Italy. "Italian" was his reply. I asked him what language was spoken in Spain. "Spanish." I asked him about languages spoken in Germany, France, Russia and Greece. He replied with German, French, Russian and Greek respectively. The implication was that they all had their own languages. Then I asked him about the language spoken in England—English, which was the case long before Columbus stumbled onto America, which he thought was India. (Of course! Why else would he call the population Indians?) That begged the question how it was America didn't have its own language: American. Also I pointed out to him that English was my third language behind Punjabi and Hindi. He was pretty much speechless, and it was interesting watching him trying to come to grips with the above statements. His comment was that Americans were improving on the archaic language spoken in England because they didn't have it right. I said that was interesting about England not getting things right. In other words using 'o' instead of zero, the sign '4 sale' instead of 'For Sale' are steps toward dramatically improving the English language. Are the above phrases serious examples of that? Pretty soon he ended the conversation and we went our separate ways.

November 3

My friends and I went to an International Club meeting at the college. I didn't want to go, but they insisted. A faculty member had just returned from a tour of Europe and the Middle East. He talked about how foreigners treated Americans in their countries, and how Americans treated foreigners in this country. The latter part was not new to me because I had experienced all that at a magnified scale. The talk lasted well over an hour, and it was one hell of a bore. I wanted to leave after that, but my friends prevailed on me to stay, and the meeting sank to the utmost bottom of boredom. I didn't know what they got out of that because the discussion and the variety show that followed were horrible, and the final program of music and dancing didn't do anything to bring up the atmosphere of hopelessness. Finally we left, and that ended a fully wasted evening.

November 5

I haven't received any letter from Dad for some time now. I wrote to him about three weeks back. A letter to Mom went out more than two weeks ago. I am wondering when they will reply. Oh well, no point in worrying about that. I will respond as and when their letters arrive. My letter to Daddy dated October eighteenth was the longest one so far. Actually I ended it prematurely because it was going to take a lot more time. I had already spent four days writing it.

Daddy finally replied to my long letter. I'm sure he was blown away by what he read, which was partly my fault because I hadn't written to him about all those problems and other routines I had run into here. I'm not sure my unloading on him the way I did was such a good idea. Here is what he wrote back:

My dear Rajinder,   October 28

I received your long letter of the eighteenth yesterday and read it three times. It was an eye-opener because the idea of life you gave us from Fort Wayne was entirely different from what I got from this letter. I was worried after reading the letter the first time, but later I was convinced with the confidence you have shown, you will glide through all those day-to-day difficulties. I'm glad at this young age of twenty you are forming such brave notions about life, and with your fighting spirit you will never let minor things upset you. You are having the experiences an average man would have between his thirties and forties. Keep it up my son—I have entire faith and confidence in you. You are forming such mature ideas about life at this young age and the means to overcome those difficulties.

I am surprised how much you have spent on the car in such a short time. It must have meant you had to work a lot harder to cover these expenses, and I'm glad your confidence has never been betrayed. Remember more reasonable speed also saves wear and tear on the car.

After reading your account of life I am not a bit worried about your financial situation. I am happy you can make ends meet.

Regarding your mention about being in the Sikh uniform, you are passing through a phase. I will leave the responsibility and decision entirely to you. To maintain this religion one has always to face some hardships in daily life. This religion is most simple, and there are very few binding rituals. You can either follow the majority or maintain your individuality. The hard days will pass. Just imagine the feeling of pride and joy in the eyes of your mother when you return in the same garb in which you left.

I have no comment to offer on the bad experience you had with your roommate. It is something one has to face in life, but one must keep one's conscience clear.

One point I missed is about the typewriter. I remember you mentioned purchasing one, and I had written back you had done well in that. I'm fine with whatever you need for your comfort and ease, provided it is within your budget. Always keep your goal in view, and you will never go wrong.

I'm blown away by your comment on my note, "There is no task that will not yield to regular patient and persistent effort." I'm glad you were able to recall it during these trying times. You never know what will surface to comfort you, and it makes my heart jump with joy that it was helpful.

Last night was Divali, but what good is Divali[4] without the family around? So I had a quiet evening reading your letter and pondering various things.

With love and affection,

Daddy

November 8

Dad's reply was wonderful, and his response was the longest letter he has ever written. He has shown supreme confidence in my ability to overcome these difficulties, which is beyond anything I could have expected. That really elevated my respect for him. The wisdom he has shown in this letter is way beyond my imagination, and he has new insight about my capabilities. He couldn't have imagined what I would be running into here, and the same would also apply to me. He picked up from my letter I had handled the situation and would continue to handle it. The confidence he has shown in my abilities has really pushed me to a

---

[4] Divali: Festival of lights celebrated in India. It symbolizes the victory of good over evil, and lamps are lit as a sign of celebration and hope for human kind.

higher level. This has given me the kick in the pants to continue on—no matter the obstacles. That was just what I needed to pull myself up by the bootstraps with a new found confidence and continue on. Any doubts I had in my mind have been erased by his letter. I'm sure it won't be smooth sailing from here on, and there will be plenty of obstacles and discrimination incidents. Then I'll remember Daddy's words, and just brush all that aside and press on.

One thing I had pointed out to him was that it was no wonder Sikh boys shave off their beards as they try to mix into this hostile society rather than remain conspicuous at the very moment they step onto the street. On this point he wrote:

"Regarding your mention about being in Sikh uniform, you are passing through a phase. I will leave the entire responsibility on you. The decision is yours."

Just imagine this coming from a father in India. He has left the responsibility of the decision entirely to me. I wonder what it would have been like if all this had been given to me in the earlier days. I don't mean in the narrow sense of shaving off, but the much broader sense of everyday life. I'm pretty sure I wouldn't have changed much of anything because who I'm has been set from years and years of training, and it's not something I can chuck out the window on a mere whim.

November 14

Finally I got a letter from Kavita after a long wait. It was just a short note to say hello and reassure me she was doing fine. She was a bit more sullen in this letter, and her handwriting was not up to par. She started the letter with, 'I miss you', and also ended it with the same phrase. She picked that up from my last letter. Again she told me to get a telephone because she is not happy being unable to talk to me.

November 22

I wrote to Kavita to thank her for her nice letter, and asking how she was doing. I reminded her that one-year anniversary of our meeting was coming up. I kept it short because she might be busy with her studies. I told her I finally had a telephone and gave her my number.

December 1

We went to a Thanksgiving Day dinner held for foreign students, and I sat there looking at the cooked bird on the table. I was quite impressed with the Americans having grown the chicken so large and wondered how they did it. One of the foreign students asked the question that was on my mind.

"How did you grow that chicken so large?"

We were deflated when they told us it was a turkey, not chicken. Needless to say there were no turkeys in India. They showed us a picture, and probably had a good laugh about us ignorant foreigners. They were asking questions about elephants, tigers and lions in India. I told them I had seen most of those animals in the Delhi Zoo. They wondered if I had ridden an elephant, and I told them I had not.

December 3

The weather was turning cold, and the fog was nothing like I had seen before. They called it Tully fog. I figured it meant you can't see two feet in front of you, but it could be a lot worse—piling snow like in Indiana.

I had been getting odd jobs, and that had kept me going. In late fall and winter there were tree pruning work available. One job was next to a field of sweet potatoes. The crop had been harvested, but there were a few of them lying around. We made a fire, and baked some for lunch. They were delicious.

Chapter 5

Roshni

(A Ray of Sunshine)

The ringing of the telephone woke me at four in the morning, and I was still half asleep when I answered it. Who could be calling at this odd hour?

"Hello."

"Hello, Rajinder. You want to guess who this is?"

I was jarred awake by Kavita's bubbly voice. "Kavita! How absolutely lovely to hear your voice. How are you doing?"

"I'm doing wonderful now that I am talking to you. Are you sitting down?"

"I'm still in bed because it's four in the morning!"

"I'm sorry about that. I have no control over what time the call goes through. Anyway, my parents and I are coming to America."

"Oh, that is wonderful! It will be delightful to see you again, assuming you are coming to California."

"Of course. Mom and I will be coming to California while Daddy takes care of business in Chicago."

"That is really exciting news. What are your plans?"

"That is what I want to know from you. We don't want to interrupt your studies. What would be a convenient time?"

Through the euphoria I managed to think about the winter break and gave her the dates.

"Good, that also fits my University schedule also. I'll get back to you about our final plans, and we'll try to visit during that time. What is the nearest major airport?"

"That would be San Francisco, California."

"I can't wait to see you. I'll ring back if there is a problem, and I am writing a letter giving you the details."

"I can't wait to see you. It will be absolutely wonderful. I will also write to you giving you details from this end."

I marveled at the turn of events. I had the telephone installed recently because she was not happy being unable to talk to me. It would have been much harder to set this up through letters.

Her letter arrived a week later. They would be flying to Chicago, and from there she would come to California with her mother. She gave me details about this trip and explained how her mother agreed to come along to America. She had been pestering her relentlessly to come to America. Finally one day her father told her he was going to America and asked if she wanted to come along with her mother. She couldn't believe her ears, and she nodded so hard her head hurt. She hugged her mother so tightly she was gasping for air. She hugged her father and didn't want to let go. Her mother asked Kavita if she had my telephone number. She nodded and her mother told her to give me a ring to find out when would be a convenient time.

Kavita instantly knew her mother had told her father about me, and she couldn't believe he had reacted the way he did. She was afraid he would have given her a dressing down of her life if he found out about me. She was sure her mother had convinced him otherwise, and she broke down as she gave her mother another hug. She ran back to the office to hug her father again and thank him. He placed the call for her because Kavita had never placed an overseas call. In the meantime she sat down to write me. Later she called me with final details about her trip to Chicago and California.

On the appointed day I was anxiously waiting for them at the San Francisco Airport. I saw Kavita, and she immediately spotted me. She told her mother to follow her as she bounded over to me, and the people in front hurriedly got out of her way. She dropped everything and locked me in a bear hug. I nodded at her mother and folded my hands behind Kavita's back in traditional Indian greeting (hands in prayer). She replied in kind. Slowly we pulled back, and I helped her pick up all her hand luggage. She wiped her tears, and I too was quite choked up. Her mother stood there mesmerized by what she had witnessed. Kavita introduced me to her mother, Meena, and I thanked her for bringing Kavita. I also expressed my condolences about her mother's passing. Meena said it was a pleasure meeting the man her daughter had traveled halfway around the world to see.

It was really something her mother thought enough of her daughter to come all this way because Kavita had told me her mother had been quite adamant she was not flying back to America. Here she had witnessed a heartwarming reunion, and I could see the love she had for her daughter. All that awed me, but mostly I was extremely happy to see

Kavita. We drove to a motel in San Bruno because I was advised that would be convenient for trips to San Francisco and other places of interest. They were fascinated with all the Christmas lights, and commented about it being along the lines of Diwali in India. The difference being Diwali is a one-night affair, but Christmas would go on for the duration of their stay.

I told them, "I had my introduction to Christmas in London."

Kavita asked, "They have Christmas in London also?"

I remembered she had arrived in London after Christmas. "Yes, they do. I asked the front desk to order a taxi to take me to the airport. I was told there were no taxis available on Christmas. They sent a driver to drop me off."

Meena said, "I vaguely remember Christmas on one of our visits there. It was a subdued affair because there was a war on at the time. I just can't imagine a taxi being unavailable on Christmas. Diwali is a huge holiday in India, and there are no such problems."

We had two adjacent rooms, and the two of them went to freshen up. I was in my room settling in when the door opened and Kavita came in. She gave me a hug after closing the door behind her. We looked into each other's eyes, and I kissed her. She pulled back and gave me a heartwarming smile.

She said, "Ooh. That was very nice. Why didn't you do that on the ship?"

"I was hoping you would take the lead. You did tell me not to let a golden opportunity pass us by. Not only that, I read something that pushed me to kiss you."

"Oh? What could that be?"

"An American author, Hemingway wrote: 'Never delay kissing a pretty girl or opening a good bottle of whiskey. Both should be investigated as quickly as possible.'"

"Oh my! Where was he when we were on the ship? Would you have kissed me if you had known that quote?"

"How could I have not? You know very well I follow orders!"

We laughed and sat down. I looked into her eyes and said, "Happy anniversary, my love."

"Oh, you remembered! Happy anniversary, Rajinder. I'm not happy you stole my line! I was hoping to be here on the tenth, but it didn't fit our schedule."

"Would have been very nice, but I had college to attend, and your being here would have really distracted me."

"I know. That was the case at my university also. Important thing is I'm here with you, and nothing else matters."

She gave me a very nice camera. I remembered her asking me if I had one. She said now I had no excuse for not sending her pictures. I thanked her and would do my best to honor her wishes. We held hands and talked about how much we missed each other. Pretty soon her mother came in and we talked about their trip.

Later Kavita was busy in the bathroom, which gave me a chance to talk to Meena.

She said, "I'm glad I came because it was wonderful to witness how happy she was to see you. I have never seen her like this before. By now you must know how she is when she has her mind set on something."

"I gathered that from the ship. Through all that time she was very considerate and wonderful to me. Although I do know you have royally spoiled her."

"She is our only child—what could we do? She knows how to get her way, and there's nothing we can do about it."

"She wrote to me you were adamant you weren't coming back to America. What changed your mind? Did she manipulate you like she always did?"

"No. She begged and pleaded, but I wouldn't budge because I was tired of the airplane journey and didn't want to go through that again. It is so noisy, and you sit there hour-after-hour with pretty much nothing to do. I can only read for so long. Also there were babies crying and children running around with no supervision. I loved the ship voyages. Kavita understood and told me she also hated the airplane journey. She would much rather travel by ship for its relaxing serenity. In this case it was just not possible because that trip would have taken four weeks each way, and her father didn't have that kind of time available.

"She finally gave up trying to convince me and lapsed into a depression. She would hardly eat or go out, and she wandered listlessly around the house. Her studies suffered because her heart was not in it. This was almost as bad as when her grandmother passed away. Her friends were missing her and asked me what had happened to her. She had been so out-going and vivacious. It broke my heart to see her that depressed. Then her father's business trip to Chicago came up, and I had to give it a serious thought. I had to make this trip for my daughter's sake."

I sat there speechless. I knew parents do all kinds of things for their children, and this one rated at the top. I had great respect for what Meena had done for her daughter and for me. She continued. "Talking about keeping her spirits up, the essay and the poem about your grandfather's passing was very helpful to all of us when my mom passed."

"I figured that might be the case because it sure helped me as I wrote it, and got me through that difficult time. I am glad it was helpful."

Meena said, "Yes, but she was upset with you,"

"I remember her being unhappy when she realized I was seventeen when I wrote it."

"Precisely. That writing helped us very much, and played an important role in my decision to come here. I wanted to meet the man who has my daughter so fascinated. Also on behalf of my family I want to thank you for being so very supportive."

We went to lunch, and they asked about what all there was to see around the area. Being a new arrival I was not very familiar with the sites. I had heard about San Francisco and the Golden Gate Bridge. Kavita wanted to see my college and also my apartment. Next morning we headed to Fresno, and I had a chance to talk to Kavita on the way. Meena was dozing in the back because the trip had tired her quite a bit. Kavita wanted to know about my plans and how long it would be before I came back to India. I told her it would be another three or four years— pretty much what I had told her on the ship.

She asked, "Are you coming for a visit to India before that?"

"It would be impossible for me to come any time soon. Daddy is in the process of building a house, so I can't ask him for money. I doubt if I could earn enough for the trip. It has been extremely tough finding decent jobs because of the discrimination problems."

"Discrimination? Here in America? That's hard to believe."

"You are right, it's hard to believe, but I'm a shining example. I went to a dozen places asking if they had a job opening. I was repeatedly told they were full up. I stopped at a fruit packinghouse and asked for a job. The foreman looked at me sympathetically and told me to come back for work the following day. Later I learned he had been a foreign student himself and knew what I was going through. I finally had a job for last summer, and I worked very hard because I didn't want to let him down."

She was horrified about what I had just told her. "Did you run into any other problems?"

"Yes, I had similar problems looking for an apartment because they didn't want to rent to a foreigner. I was turned down at a lot of places, and a Mexican co-worker helped me get a place."

She was not too happy when she heard all this. "Why didn't you write to me about this?"

"I didn't want to burden you because it would just have upset you, and there was nothing anyone could have done. Besides, you had enough problems of your own. Only my daddy knew about the discrimination."

"Why didn't you pack up and come back to India if you were having all these difficulties?"

"Kavita, my family has invested heavily in my coming here, and I'm determined to see it through. I'm not going to be defeated by these Americans."

I asked her about her routines in India. She said it was pretty much college work and some socializing with her friends and classmates. "I met girls from rural areas and had taken it on myself to help them. My parents were very supportive, and the girls were really appreciative because they had never been away from home."

I said, "It sure would have been nice if you had been in town to help me during my first few months at the boarding school. I hadn't been away from home, and I was on my own at the tender age of seven."

"I wish I'd been there to take care of you."

We laughed. She would have been all of ten at the time. She kissed me after checking to make sure her mother was asleep. We arrived at my apartment. I had straightened it out the best I could before I left. I had them sit at the dining table because those were the only chairs we had. I made tea and pulled out snacks I had set aside for this occasion. They were fascinated with the place—a small one-bedroom unit, but it was just fine for the time being because we spent so little time there. Most of the time we were either attending classes or out on odd jobs. All of our studying we did at the library where we had all those books at our disposal. We didn't have any reference materials at home.

Meena took pictures and we sat there talking for a while because she needed a break from traveling. We drove to the college, and there was not much activity because it was winter break. We went to the library, and Kavita wanted to see a book on electrical engineering. She was fascinated with the pictures of the electrical equipment and the

116

circuitry. She wanted me to explain one of the diagrams. I tried to, but I lost her after five seconds. I showed them the electrical engineering lab, and all we could do was peek inside. She was quite fascinated with the room, and one wall was a large electrical distribution system. There were generators, motors and other apparatus visible. She asked me if I knew what all that equipment was. I told her I could run most of it.

Kavita was getting bored, and she asked about an Indian restaurant for lunch. She was not happy when I told her there was none in town. I said the only way she could have Indian food was if she cooked. She gave me a dirty look and asked me if I was trying to make fun of her. Meena laughed and said her daughter didn't know how to cook. I enjoyed the moment, and said the only other way was if I cooked. Kavita brightened up, but Meena told her she shouldn't be putting me to work like that. I said it was not really a big problem. Only thing was it would take some time, and they both offered to help. I said I was not very good at it and would not be able to compete with the cooks they had in India. They said anything would be better than all the western food they had been eating since leaving India. I went to work after we picked up some groceries. Kavita asked what she could do, and I told her to peel and chop an onion. She was barely able to peel it, and I took it from her. I asked her to wash and chop the vegetables. I got the onion chopped, and she was thankful she didn't have to do that job.

I called Maldev and invited him to join us for lunch. That would give him a chance to meet Kavita. He declined and told me to have fun—especially with her mother there. He snickered and hung up.

The lunch was basic Indian vegetarian food. Meena was fascinated and commented about my being in constant motion. I told her it was a necessity as we had very little time to do the cooking. Also we made large quantities so we wouldn't have to cook as often. Kavita was trying to help the best she could. Mostly I told her to do the stirring. She got carried away and almost splashed herself. I didn't have an apron so I tied a towel around her waist. Meena was really enjoying the scene and took pictures. Kavita was not happy, but she was a good sport. I had Meena take pictures with the camera Kavita had given me. They enjoyed the meal, and Meena complimented Kavita about pitching in and helping with clean up.

They decided to stay the night in a hotel in Fresno so we could see the sights in the area. Meena booked two adjacent rooms. I told her that was not necessary since I could easily drive back to my place, but Meena said Kavita would want me nearby. She agreed whole-heartedly and overrode me. Meena said it was time for a nap, and they went to their room. I settled in my room to look at some of my paperwork that needed attention. A bit later Kavita came in, and I asked her why she wasn't taking a nap. She said there would be plenty of time for naps after she left here. In the meantime she wasn't going to waste our precious time together.

Kavita asked about going to Disneyland because one of her friends back in India had been there and said it was lots of fun. I had heard it was in the Los Angeles area and checked with the clerk at the front desk. She told me it was past Los Angeles and would be about six to seven hours' drive. I figured it would be another ten to twelve hours' drive to get back to San Bruno after spending one day in Disneyland. Kavita was quite excited about that, and I showed her the roads (US 99 and 101) we would be taking. Her friend had shown her pictures of the place and had told her about the rides. I told Kavita her mother might not be able to handle a seven-hour trip to Disneyland and another ten to twelve hour drive back to San Bruno. She thought about it and reluctantly agreed with me. I was happy she put her mother first. Meena had already done so much for us by coming to California. We got back from coffee and went to check on Meena. She was wondering where we had been. Kavita told her she had decided to skip her nap to spend time with me. She also told her about the trip to Disneyland. I could tell Meena was not too thrilled about seventeen hours on the road. Kavita told her she had figured that, and I had talked her out of it. Meena smiled and gave me an approving nod.

The following day we drove to Kings Canyon National Park. They were asking what the trip was about, and I told them it was about trees. Kavita was rather perplexed. "You mean we are going there to see trees?" I told her to reserve her judgment until she saw them. She seemed a bit miffed, and said she would rather have gone shopping. I told her I was fully aware of her zeal for shopping. I was told San Francisco would be the place for that and had planned accordingly. In the meantime she was stuck going to the Park. We arrived there, and Kavita was still displeased, but she was a bit more cheerful because she had resigned herself to this. We walked to the redwood trees I had seen on my previous visit. They stood there awestruck at the sight of the giant Sequoias. I knew exactly what they were feeling, for I also felt the same way when I saw them.

The Sequoia trees stand over two hundred feet tall and could be a couple of thousand years old, which would make them some of the oldest living things on Earth. We walked around, and the whole atmosphere was so peaceful and serene. There was a gentle breeze, and the sun was out in full force. They were both quiet as they took it all in. We took pictures and Meena took a picture of Kavita and me looking up to the top of the tree. We decided to have refreshments at a stand we had passed on our way in. Kavita was again her bubbly self and apologized for being difficult on the way to the Park. She said the place was so peaceful and was glad she came. I told her I was ready to leave her behind at the motel and hoped she was glad I didn't. She gave me a big hug and commented, "Try that and see how far you'll get!"

Meena was enjoying all this and told me her daughter would always change her mind as soon as she got to the destination. That was the way she pretty much behaved, and Kavita was not pleased. She said to her mother, "Why are you telling him this?" She gave her mother a stern look. Meena just laughed and told her to behave.

On the drive back to San Bruno Meena was dozing. I asked Kavita further details about how this trip came about. What Meena had told me about why she changed her mind about coming to America made a lot of sense, but I felt there had to be more to it. Kavita was silent for a few moments trying to pull her thoughts together. Then she replied, "I asked Mom about this trip and how Daddy reacted when he found out about you. Mom did not want to say, but I pressed her, and she finally relented."

Meena told her, 'We returned to India because your grandmother had a heart attack. Kavita, you ate like a bird and not your usual talkative self. Often you excused yourself before we finished dinner, and you listlessly moped around the house for weeks. I didn't know what to say so I told your father you probably were just going through a phase and would snap out of it. Also it might have something to do with your grandmother passing away. Your father was not pacified and kept bringing up the subject. Finally I had to tell him the truth.'

Meena told her daddy, "Our daughter met a tall, handsome young man on the ship, and she was infatuated with him. He was easy to talk to, and she was very comfortable around him. They had relaxed conversations without any undercurrents and were very respectful toward each other. On top of that she had never seen an Indian young man as tall as him, and she stole away as often as she could to spend time with him. I had inkling about what was going on, but felt it was just a minor shipboard fling and it would pass. I didn't know what to say to you so I said nothing."

Her daddy's reply shocked them both. He said to Meena, "I knew about him. I caught a glimpse of Kavita talking with a tall young man, and I asked a steward to find out what was going on. I was told she was spending time with a young man named Rajinder. I told the steward to let me know of any misbehavior by him or her. After all, she's my only child, and I have the responsibility to protect her."

In my shocked surprise I almost shouted, "Your father knew about us?" Meena stirred in the backseat. Kavita hushed me and said she didn't want to wake her mother.

"Yes, he did. Let me continue."

Her mom asked her daddy, "Why didn't you tell me you knew?"

Daddy asked, "Why didn't you tell me what was going on?"

Meena said to her father, "I was trying to figure out what to say or how to approach you. She wanted to go to Indiana to be with him, and I prayed to God to help work things out. I knew how much she liked him and wanted to be with him. I think Rajinder felt the same way about our daughter. We were planning to go to Indiana while you were visiting Washington, DC. It all became moot when we had to rush back to India.

Kavita said, "He was not happy Mom knew, but he respected her silence because I had confided in her. I had asked for her help in being able to spend time with you in America."

This is what he said to Kavita. "There were a lot of hours to kill on the ship. I knew you'd be bored and might do something stupid. I had to know what you were up to. I breathed a sigh of relief after I saw you with Rajinder and how he was with you. I had seen him with his daddy before we boarded the ship."

She was surprised and said to her daddy, "You were watching Rajinder before we got on the ship?"

Her daddy said, 'Kavita, I saw you watching Rajinder before we boarded the ship. I was pretty sure his daddy was an army officer, which reassured me when I saw you two together on the ship. I somehow knew you would be safe with him. I figured it was a minor infatuation that would pass when we left the ship in Genoa. I never dreamed it would lead to this. I should have guessed otherwise, though. I saw you when you came back to the cabin on the last night before Genoa. You had tears running down your cheeks, plopped yourself on the bed without changing, and I heard your muffled sobbing and crying. I wanted to sit with you and comfort you, but I couldn't. That was one of the more difficult moments of my life."

Kavita continued, "I couldn't believe what I was hearing. My father seemed so aloof, yet he was being kind and really understanding. I couldn't believe he was paying such close attention to me."

"He told me, 'Don't forget, I took you along wherever we went. If I hadn't, you wouldn't have been on that ship to meet him, and we wouldn't be talking about it. I have a business trip to Chicago coming up. From there you can travel to California with your mother while I take care of business in Washington.'

"I was stunned and incredulous at what I was hearing. I flung my arms around Daddy's neck and thanked him profusely. Rajinder, I hope this explains how this visit came about."

I was dumbfounded, and my mouth dropped open because I had trouble believing what she was telling me. I was very sure it was not easy for her father. Most probably his first reaction would have been to put a stop to it and forbid her to see me, which would have been a normal reaction of an Indian father. How he went from that to bringing her here was beyond me. I was sure Meena had something to do with it. I could see how much they loved Kavita, and I was truly grateful for all they did to bring us together. We got back to the motel and went to bed early after an early dinner.

I had done some checking about the area and had planned trips to show them the sights. Next morning we went to Telegraph Hill lookout point in San Francisco where they had a breath-taking view of the city. From there we went to Fisherman's Wharf where we had a leisurely look around. They did some shopping, and we had lunch there. Meena asked me about a big boat that had just pulled up. I asked the waiter and he told us it was a ferryboat, and you could tour the Bay. Kavita was quite excited and asked her mother if we could go on it. That turned out to be a very enjoyable trip. The boat went under the Golden Gate Bridge for a wonderful view. Kavita was busy taking pictures and having a good time. Meena loved being on the boat, and I'm sure it brought back memories of all her voyages. She sat down and enjoyed the ride. Kavita and I walked to the bow and talked about the ship voyage that seemed so long ago. A little later she got serious and turned to me.

She said, "I knew you were very mature for a nineteen-year-old when we were together on the ship. I'm quite impressed how much this year in America has changed you."

"I appreciate your comment. Life has a way of pushing you along. I have been through a lot during the last year, and it's bound to have influenced me."

"That is an understatement. All you told me on our drive to Fresno really had me worried. Now I know I have nothing to worry about because you have become a very confident young man."

I shrugged my shoulders and replied, "I'm doing the best I can. It is all up to me, and there's no one I can turn to for advice or help. My parents and family are not here for me to lean on. I had no idea what I was getting myself into when I embarked on this journey to America. You also have been very helpful through this year."

She was surprised. "Me? How can that be? I have been nothing but a pain. I was wondering how I would have reacted if I had been involved with someone with problems similar to mine. I'm not sure I could have been as supportive. You have been the one constant in my life and helped me through this year. You kept writing to me even though I was sporadic in my replies. You wrote to me about your grandfather's passing and how you understood what I was going through. I re-read your letters whenever I felt really down, especially what you wrote about his passing."

We got back to the dock. I asked around for the way to the Golden Gate Bridge, and we arrived there after getting lost. The bridge looked so majestic, and it was not engulfed in mist like my previous visit. We took a long walk on the bridge, and Meena was quite impressed with the whole experience. She asked Kavita if she was enjoying herself. She looked at me and said she was enjoying herself tremendously. Meena smiled and just shook her head.

By this time I could see Meena was quite tired. She was used to resting in the afternoon, and this was the second day she had not been able to nap. Kavita also looked tired. We got back to the motel and the two of them went to their room. I went to my room and sat down to study and make notes in my journal.

There was a discrete knock on my door, and Kavita walked into my room.

"Kavita, I thought you were tired."

"Yes I am, but I'm too excited to sleep. Why aren't you lying down for a nap?"

"I have gotten out of the habit because there just isn't any time for naps. I'm too busy with college, housework, homework and part-time jobs. I had to stop taking naps after I arrived in California.

"In Indiana you still took naps?"

"Yes, I did, but not regularly. Some days I had classes in the afternoon."

"I don't know what I'd do if I couldn't take my nap."

"I had similar thoughts in the beginning, but now I don't even think of taking a nap."

She sat on my lap, and we kissed. She looked into my eyes and said, "I'm sorry I was so harsh about your drive across the country."

"Kavita, you have no reason to apologize because you had every right to be upset. I was careless and deserved your displeasure. That is exactly what I wrote to you in my response."

"Yes, that's true. Just like you wrote in your letter, we are very much alike. An average Indian woman wouldn't have behaved the way I did on the ship. I must have confused you in the beginning."

"That's a huge understatement. I must have liked it otherwise we wouldn't be sitting here talking about it. Despite that there were some boundaries we couldn't cross."

She asked, "For example?"

"Kissing!"

"Yes. I was upset you didn't kiss me on our last night on the ship."

"I can understand. You had been taking the lead through most of our relationship. So why didn't you kiss me if that's what you wanted?"

"For the same reason you didn't kiss me. Those boundaries held me back. My way of thinking was, 'would be nice if he kisses me.'"

I said, "That is funny. I was thinking 'would be nice if she kisses me!'"

She said, "That's hilarious! So you kissed me the first opportunity we got. Anyway, getting back to your driving. You are what you are, and I'm sure you are more experienced now, but just don't do anything like that with Mom along. Okay?"

"Kavita, I wouldn't do that even if I'm by myself. Besides, the speed limit in California is sixty five."

"You mean your promise not to do hundred miles an hour was pretty much a hollow one?"

"In a way, because a speeding ticket would drain my bank account. I couldn't afford it!"

"You mean you knew that when you told me you wouldn't be going that fast anymore?"

"Yes, and I saw no reason to bore you with the details."

She said, "I'm not happy. Here I thought you were being very considerate about my feelings. Come to find out you were only concerned with the cost of the ticket!"

"You are the main reason I haven't driven that fast and don't have any desire to either. Does it matter if there is a secondary reason?"

She kissed me, "No. That I really appreciate."

"See? You do have a major influence over me."

"As you do over me. It's good we keep each other in line."

She wanted to know what I was writing.

"I'm putting down my thoughts on your visit and what all we have been doing. I want to have this as a wonderful reminder. Also I'm writing a letter to Dad."

"Nice. That is quite a big folder of letters."

"I'm looking through Dad's letters to see what questions I need to answer and what all I have already addressed."

"Interesting. What are those carbon copies in that stack?"

I said, "Those are copies of my letters to Dad."

She was blown away. "What? You keep copies of your letters to your dad? Who in his right mind keeps copies of letters to anyone?"

"Well, you have a living example right in front of you. Dad always has a lot of questions about what is going on with me. Sometimes our exchange of letters is not sequential. In other words I would write to him before getting his next letter and vice versa. I figured this was the only way to make sure all his questions were answered."

She was blown away. "Looks like you have all angles covered. There are a lot of letters back and forth. Is there one of special significance?"

"Oh yes, there is. I wrote him a very long letter detailing all the discrimination problems I've been going through here, and also about problems I had finding work and a place to live."

"I remember your talking about that. Can I read it?"

I pulled the October 18th letter out of the file folder and handed it to her. She was absolutely blown away with my filing system—letters to Mom, Dad and brother interspersed with my letters to them. She took the letter and went to her room to read it. She came back and sat on my lap with tears in her eyes. She said her mom wanted to read the letter after she saw how it affected her. Meena came in some time later and put the letter on the table. She said, "Wow, Rajinder. What a huge battle you've had over the last year you have been here. Yet you carry on as if it is just another day and we never would have guessed what all you've been through."

I replied, "Well, I have been through a lot over my twenty-year life. Dad has been in the army and we were moving every so often. Then I was in the boarding school which was quite a challenge, but I managed to survive that. Then I arrived here—right into the buzz saw of discrimination and hatred hurled at me. Luckily my upbringing prepared me for some of that, although there really was no preparing for anything of this nature."

Meena said, "I don't see how you are still standing tall after all that you've been through. I'm quite concerned about you. Aren't you worried about what all lies ahead of you?"

"To a certain extent, but I have a feeling I've weathered the worst of the storm and am confident I'll be able to continue on. Let's face it; I really have no choice in this matter. I'm a born optimist, and I feel it will pass. Sure beats sitting in a corner crying about the unfairness of it all."

They were not pacified, but accepted my optimistic attitude. Kavita and I went for a walk. We talked about pictures she had taken. I asked, "You are going to send me some of those pictures, aren't you?"

She said teasingly, "Of course I will send you pictures! You will have to write to me asking for them."

"You don't have to put it that way. I have written to you—often. Most of the time you were the one lax about writing back."

Her demeanor changed. "I'm sorry. Please don't remind me."

"I didn't want this sounding like it did. I know you were going through tough times after your grandmother's passing. I sure did when my grandfather passed away. My studies suffered because I was listless most of the time."

"It was like that for me except I didn't have studies to distract me. In a way studies might have helped me get through my loss. Let's not dwell on it because that's in the past, and I'm feeling a lot better now that I'm with you."

"I'm also feeling a lot better having you here. It's wonderful even though we know it is only for a short time."

She was quite appreciative, "Yes, and I want to thank you for taking the time off from your busy schedule to be with me."

"You really think I would have done otherwise? Luckily I don't have a steady job because that might have posed a problem."

She again thanked me for being so helpful through her ordeal over the previous year.

I said, "I'm glad. I was really worried about you after your telephone call telling me about your grandmother having a heart attack, and you were really devastated. Then the letters you posted from London and Istanbul really had me concerned because I had a pretty good idea what you were going through. One part of you wanted to be with me, while the other part wanted to be with your grandmother. Not only that, you were apologizing for having to run back to India. Stuff like that only happened in movies. This was real life, and I was deeply touched by what you wrote. What could I do except help you through your grief and try to keep your spirits up? I had no experience in this and did what I thought was best. I'm glad it was helpful."

Kavita looked very appreciative. "Now you understand why I had to come. I wanted to thank you personally because a letter wouldn't have sufficed. You know I'm not a good writer, and I'm certainly glad you write well. I appreciated what you wrote, and it was extremely helpful."

"It looks like we helped each other, and it brought you here. What more could I ask?"

We were looking into each other's eyes. Suddenly I blurted out, "Roshni."

"What do you mean, Roshni?"

"That is my name for you."

She furrowed her brows and said, "I have a perfectly good name—Kavita. I love this name."

"I'm sure you do and so do I."

"Then why would I want a new name?"

"Would you allow me to explain? I have been going through all kinds of problems here, and these have been rather dark times for me. Then you arrived and brought a ray of sunshine into my life. What would you call it?"

She smiled and said, "Roshni!"

"Well?"

She gave me a kiss and said, "I approve, and I feel the same. I have been going through dark times, too, and you brightened my life so much, but I don't think 'Roshni' fits you."

"You can call me anything you want."

I could see her demeanor had changed to something more serious. I braced myself for some serious questions.

She looked at me and said, "We need to talk about other serious things."

"Yes, we do. You start."

"I had a feeling you would say that."

"In other words, you know me better than I thought."

She began pensively, "It's been a year since our meeting."

I interjected, "And a wonderful meeting it was, wasn't it?"

"Yes, it was. And don't distract me. You have done that in the past, and you are very good at that. For example, you start kissing me when you don't want to answer my question."

"Sorry. I won't interrupt."

"I didn't say don't interrupt. I said don't distract me. Anyway it has been a very eventful year. You have been here working very hard, and I have been there mostly moping."

I took her hand and said, "You had a very good reason to be moping. Losing your grandmother was a huge blow."

"Yes, it was, but that was not the only reason for my moping. In between I was thinking about you. I remember what all you told me on the ship. It has been a year since you arrived here and seems like it will be another three or more years before you finish and return to India."

"Yes, that is pretty much true. I have been counting the days, too. This is something I have to do, and there's no getting around that."

"I know, and I admire you for that. That doesn't change the fact I am miserable in India without you."

I squeezed her hand and added, "If it is any consolation, I'm miserable here without you. I don't see any way we can change our situation. You can't stay here, and I can't leave before I graduate. We are in quite a quandary."

"I know. I'm dreading the trip back to India."

"I'm not looking forward to your leaving either. I have racked my brain trying to come up with something to resolve our situation. Only thing that accomplished was a headache."

She smiled, "You have the knack of interjecting humor no matter what the subject. That is what I like about you."

"I thought the mood needed lightening. This is heavy stuff we are talking about. No matter what happens, I have a feeling we won't like the outcome."

"Why do you say that?"

"Kavita, three years is a very long time, and I can't expect you to sit there moping. I have a feeling somewhere along the way you will get angry at our situation. I don't know how your parents would feel about this long wait. I know they love you very much, and I'm absolutely shocked at your father's reaction when he found out about me. Your mother came all this way so we could be together. I'm so impressed with your parents and also very jealous."

She was surprised and said, "What do you have to be jealous about? Look at your situation. I have been asking in India if a mother would let her nineteen-year-old son to take off alone to America. None of them would allow that, but your mother let you follow your dream. Your parents supported you, and you have told me about the wonderful letters you have been exchanging with your father. The letter you wrote to him about your trip to California was a gem, as was your letter I just read. I can't imagine being able to talk to my father at that level."

"We both have wonderful parents. Coming here was quite a sacrifice your mother made for you and me. I can see the trip has been hard on her, and she tires easily as we go running about. Take good care of her when you get back because she'll be exhausted."

"Thank you for mentioning that. I admit I haven't been paying attention, and I'll be more attentive."

"She deserves no less. I'm doing what I can, but most of that has to come from her daughter."

"You are right."

I said, "Regarding my trip to America, this is not my first long distance adventure."

"Oh yes? What else do I need to know about you?"

"I was eleven. It was the start of summer vacation. I checked myself out of the boarding school and took a rickshaw to the train station. At my destination I got off the train and found my way to the bus stand. I rode the bus to a village near my village, and had to hoof it from there. I had to go through a village along the way. The village I arrived at I didn't recognize. I asked a nice lady the name of the village, and my fears were confirmed—I was lost. Apprehensively I asked if she knew the way to my village. She pointed me to a path, and I arrived at my village, but didn't know the way to our house from that side. A kindly gentleman saw I was lost and escorted me to Grandpa's house."

"All that when you were eleven? And your parents let you do that. Wow, I'm impressed. Anyway, we still have a problem."

"Yes we do. You have seen quite a bit of my life here. It's not easy, and it has been quite challenging for me to adjust. I never had a job in my life, and keeping house was not something I had to do in India. Again, I had to adjust. If I keep adjusting like this my back will be tied in knots. Like I said, I have another three or more years to go. At that point I don't know what the situation will be."

She got up and sat on my lap. Warm and tingly energy flowed through my body as we kissed. It was a feeling of aliveness that sent shudders up and down my spine. I was aroused by her kisses, her embrace, her body fragrance, and she giggled as she felt me poking at her. She gyrated her hips while looking into my eyes. I was embarrassed, and she loved it. She kissed me passionately while pressing her breasts hard against me. I put one hand on her breast and the other under her behind.

"Oh, you remembered."

"Of course! You think I would forget something like that? I also remember something else that followed."

She smiled, pulled her skirt up, and I got my hand on her naked behind. We fondled each other, and her smile was luminous. After a while we heard noises from next door, and we were disappointed as she got off my lap. She turned around and pulled her skirt up to flash her behind. I turned her around and kissed her while fondling her behind and breast. She gave me a faint smile. I sat down at the desk, and she sat on the chair nearby. Meena walked in and asked how we were doing. Kavita recounted some of the things we had been talking about. Meena wanted to take a walk after her nap. I checked at the office, and they directed me to a park not too far away. We enjoyed the walk and started thinking about dinner. They wanted to know about Indian restaurants in the area. I told her the nearest one was in San Francisco, but they didn't want to drive back there again and we settled for a restaurant nearby. After dinner we sat around and watched television. I was lost since I didn't have a television and didn't know what programs were on at what time. They settled on a movie, and after that we turned in.

The next day we went to the Winchester Mystery House in San Jose. It is a huge house built by Sara Winchester, widow of William Winchester who invented the Winchester rifle. Here is what the brochure had to say about the place:

"Sarah Winchester was deeply saddened by the death of her husband. Her daughter, Annie had died fifteen years earlier. She consulted a psychic who told Sarah thousands of people had died because of the rifles manufactured by her husband, and their spirits were seeking vengeance."

There were different versions of what all had transpired. The net result was she had to continue adding to the house to keep the spirits confused, which would keep her safe.

They enjoyed the tour. Kavita thought they had a big house, but in comparison this one was huge. She could have all kinds of fun in a house that size, but she would be afraid to play hide and seek with her friends. They would all get lost and never be seen again. Kavita wanted to know where we were going next. I told her we could go to Santa Cruz beach and have lunch there. She had not been to a beach before and was interested. While we were out of earshot of Meena I explained the beach attire to Kavita and asked if it would be a problem for either of them. She looked at me with amusement and asked if that was the reason I went to the beach. I told her I had been to the beach once, and that was at the suggestion of my old classmate, Sib.

"Did you enjoy it?"

"I'm not going to lie to you. Of course, I enjoyed it."

"Is that the normal beach attire?"

"It is."

"Is there anything else I should know?"

"Are you sure you want to know?"

She thought for a moment and nodded rather apprehensively. By that time Meena rejoined us, and we figured we would continue our conversation at a later time. Kavita told her mother what I had said about the beach. Meena knew all about beach attire because she had been to the beaches in England during her trips there. She hadn't been to beaches in America, but figured it couldn't be too different. We drove to Santa Cruz and went for lunch. Meena excused herself to go to the restroom as we sat down.

Kavita asked, "All right. What were you going to tell me earlier when we were interrupted by my mother?"

"I'm afraid to tell you."

"I'm not going to let you off the hook. Come on, tell me."

"You will be upset."

By this time she was impatient, "Come on. You are not going to leave me hanging like this."

"Okay, you asked for it. It was during my very early days here. My friend, Khanna had been here a bit longer. He knew I enjoyed ice cream, and he got me ice cream like I never had before."

"That was it? What a letdown."

"No, that was not it."

"Sorry, go on."

"He took me to a newsstand and showed me a Playboy magazine. In the center of it was a folded picture of a woman."

She seemed to relax. "That must have been nice. What did she look like?"

"The woman was naked."

"Naked? I'm sorry. I didn't mean to shout."

"You had every right to be startled. I hope you realize I had no idea what the magazine was about, but that is what guys do to each other. He knew it would shock me, and he was right."

"I believe you. Did you buy the magazine?"

I shook my head. "No, I didn't."

"And why not?"

"I couldn't afford it."

"So you missed out?"

"Not really. Playboy is a monthly magazine."

"And it has a picture of a naked woman every month?"

"Yes it does. Different women every month."

"Different women every month?"

I was feeling rather sorry I brought up this subject. "Yes, there are pictures of more than one naked woman in there."

She was amused by my discomfort. "I can see why you wanted to come to this country."

"Of course, I couldn't get anything like that in India. I saw it all in my dream and decided to come here—the land of Playboy magazine."

We both laughed. We saw Meena coming back and got serious in a hurry. After lunch we walked out to the arcade, and Meena was not happy about all the noise. We walked out to the beach, and I asked Meena if it was pretty much the same as England. She said it was except for, "That one." She pointed at a girl in a bikini. I had not seen that during my previous visit. Kavita was wide-eyed and couldn't believe what she saw. Meena asked if we could go someplace quieter for a walk. I asked around and was told about Sunset Beach near Watsonville. They gave me directions, and we drove there. It was very quiet compared to the beach in Santa Cruz, and we went for a long walk.

Later we were driving back to San Bruno, and the radio was playing. Kavita was not exactly thrilled about American music, but there was no other choice. I had the volume turned down because Meena was dozing. A song caught both our attention. It was a woman singing about a six-foot tall lifeguard who had golden tan and was very handsome.

Dark and handsome, golden tan

Six feet tall, man oh man![5]

Evidently she had a crush on him. Kavita was quite surprised and looked at me while the phrase was sung. She snickered and said, "You've

---

[5]   You can listen to the song at: [that is a zero after C] youtube.com: watch?v/C0JK4yPSgkU

been here a year and they already have a song about you on the radio. Have you been working as a lifeguard on the side?"

I played along. "Of course, I told them you were coming and I wanted this song on the radio immediately. You didn't know I had this much pull with those radio stations!"

She laughed. "You did a great job directing the recording."

By this time I was laughing, too. "Yes. They wanted me to come to Hollywood for the recording, but I was too busy getting ready for your arrival and told them to come to my place. I forgot to show you the gold plated record they gave me!"

"Right! I fully understand how something that minor would slip your mind!"

"Of course. You had me thoroughly distracted. I had to do the cooking and cleaning. Lucky I remembered my way back."

We had a good laugh, and she snuggled up closer with her head on my shoulder. We got back to San Bruno after an eventful day. I'm sure there was a lot more I could have showed them, but I really didn't know the area, and I relied on friends to guide me. One thing they mentioned was a tree two hundred miles north of San Francisco where you could drive through it. That sounded intriguing, and I talked to Kavita and Meena. I showed them the map, and it would be an all-day trip.

The following morning we headed to Leggett. It was pleasant drive through San Francisco on Highway 101. Meena was in the back reading. Kavita and I were talking most of the way. She wanted to know all about my experiences since I got here, and I explained the best I could. Mostly she wanted to know more about discrimination. We talked about similar problems in India and the prevalence of discrimination there. She didn't understand and asked me to explain. I told her the caste system precluded people from getting ahead. She agreed with me, but told me things were changing. I told her I was fully aware of that. When Daddy moved out of the village he took two families with him. They were from the lowest rung of the ladder, and they did very well under his guidance. The men found work outside, and their wives were helping Mom take care of our household. Their kids were educated and had moved on. I was very proud of Daddy for doing that.

We drove through the tree at Leggett, and they took a lot of pictures. Meena tried to look for the top of the tree and almost lost her balance. Luckily Kavita was nearby to steady her. On the way back we stopped at the Indian restaurant in San Francisco. We enjoyed the dinner, and the ride back to San Bruno was very pleasant. Kavita mentioned the only thing missing was Indian music. I told her I had a radio in Indiana, and we were able to get Indian music on Radio Ceylon. I left it there for my friends because I wasn't sure I would be able to get that Indian radio station in California.

The following morning we took it easy. After a leisurely breakfast we headed to San Francisco for the shopping mother and daughter were interested in. We went to Union Square shopping center and walked through a lot of stores. They said the shopping centers in Virginia were nothing like these in California. Kavita was going through clothes racks and she picked out several dresses. The sales lady directed her to the dressing room, and Kavita handed me her purse. I gave her a dirty look for having me hold it for her. Luckily I managed to fit it in a bag I had. I could see Meena looking around in another section. Kavita looked lovely as she tried on the dresses, which reminded me of our time on the ship. More often than not she would be in a different dress in the evening.

A few minutes later she came out wearing a strapless blue dress. It was a bit short for her, and the top barely covered her full breasts. She had tied her long flowing hair out of the way, and she walked toward me with regal grace as if the dress had taken control of her. The only thing missing was a tiara, and I was awestruck. Blue was her favorite color, and she was wearing a baby blue sari when I first saw her on the gangplank in Bombay.

"How do I look?"

I was speechless because I had never seen her in anything like that dress, and she looked stunning. I pulled out the camera and took several pictures of her posing for me. I found my voice and told her how beautiful she looked. Meena saw me taking pictures and came over. She agreed Kavita looked wonderful, but didn't like the dress because it was too revealing. Kavita asked my opinion, but said, "Never mind" when she saw the look on my face. Meena told her to put the dress back. Kavita asked me if she should do what her mother told her. I said I was staying out of their mother/daughter argument.

She said, "Smart decision. I already know what you are thinking."

She told her mother she'd put the dress back. They didn't have it in her size, and she knew she couldn't wear it in India. Meena was pacified, shook her head and wandered off. Kavita came over to me for a hug. She turned me around so we were up against a wall on one side. She pushed the top off her breast on that side and put my hand on her bare breast. I gave it a quick squeeze and she pushed her dress back up. She gave me a very mischievous smile and released me.

She had decided on a couple of dresses and saw me admiring a bikini on a mannequin. She had an amused look on her face and asked what I was thinking. I told her I was imagining how she would look in one. She picked one identical to what I was looking at and went to try it on. I was hoping she wouldn't come out wearing it, although I sure wanted to see her in it. She did not, but managed to get my attention from the dressing area.

"Where's my mother?"

"She is on the other side of the store."

She had a very mischievous look on her face. She was behind a wall and only I could see her. She dropped the dress she was holding in front of her revealing the bikini.

"Kavita!"

She looked perplexed and asked, "Don't you like it?"

"That is not the point. Please put your dress back on!"

She stood there baffled, "I thought you'd like it."

"I love it."

"A-ha. That's what I thought. You saw that woman on the beach with this swimsuit. Why didn't you tell her to put her clothes on?"

"Right. You really think I should have done that? I love seeing you in this bikini. Please put your clothes on before your mother sees you. You know she will blame me for this."

"You've got a point. I'll tell her it was all my doing."

"She won't believe you. She will assume I put you up to this."

She saw her opening. "Well, didn't you?"

"Not really. I only said, 'I'm imagining what you would look like.' There is a huge difference. Imagining is not putting you up to this."

"I was only trying to see if I lived up to what you were imagining."

"Actually you have surpassed anything I could have imagined. Now please put your dress on before your mother comes back. Need I remind you about the blue dress she thought was too revealing? She'll go ballistic if she sees you in this bikini."

She was still playing the mischievous game. "Where's my mom now?"

"She is still on the other side of the store."

"Keep an eye on her because I'm going to enjoy wearing this as long as I can. I love seeing you miserable and at the same time loving it. I saw you looking at the woman in the bikini in Santa Cruz. I figure I'd garner some of that attention for myself."

The sales lady was listening and couldn't help interjecting, "She does look absolutely gorgeous in this—just like she did in that blue dress she had on earlier."

"You don't have to tell me that. She looks lovely in anything she wears. She is just trying to get me into trouble. Meena is liable to shoot me if she sees her in this. There is no way I can convince her mother I didn't put her up to it."

Kavita was still being mischievous. "In a way you really did."

"Let me ask the sales lady. If I said to you I was imagining what you would look like in that bikini, would you run to put it on?"

The sales lady said, "I would if you were my boyfriend!"

They had a good laugh at my expense. She told the sales lady to let her know if her mother was coming back. She would buy the bikini, and she wanted it wrapped discretely so her mother wouldn't see it.

She turned to me. "Wouldn't you like to do something before I put my clothes on?"

I was flustered by this question. "Like what?"

"Take pictures!"

"Oh yes, pictures. Why didn't I think of that?"

She proceeded to pose for me. She kept clowning around and mocking me while I kept an eye on Meena. I saw she had bought something and was at a cash register. The sales lady said her mother was coming back, and Kavita jumped and ran into the dressing room to change. The saleslady commented how lovely my girlfriend looked. I liked the sound of that word, girlfriend. In the meantime Meena had turned around and moved to another part of the store. The saleslady saw I was holding the large bag in front of me. She looked around and there were no other customers in the store. She asked if I would like a few minutes with my girlfriend. I nodded awkwardly, and she told me to wait behind the wall, and she would warn us if anyone approached. She smiled and winked at me as I went behind the wall.

Kavita came out of the stall and was surprised to see me standing there. I told her the saleslady would warn us when her mother or anyone else approached. We embraced, but she didn't like the bag I was holding in front of me. She yanked it out of my hands and put it on the floor. She put her arms around my waist and pulled herself to me hard. I tried to bend my waist back, but to no avail. She pushed me against the wall and kissed me passionately. This was a prolonged kiss unlike the short ones earlier. She remembered the blowing on the ear trick from the ship and proceeded to do that. I was getting more and more aroused—if that was possible.

"Kavita, please!"

She laughed, pressed harder and put my hand on her breast. I fondled it and squeezed her butt with my other hand. After a while the saleslady told us Meena was coming back, and we hastily pulled apart. She told Kavita to go out to the sales floor and took me to a door that led to the restrooms. She said I could come out the other door that led to the sales area. I walked into the restroom unsteadily and splashed cold water on my face. I waited a few minutes to allow the excitement to wear off. I came out and she asked, "All forgiven?"

"Kavita, there is nothing to forgive. I'm stunned by your actions. You are something else."

I asked her where she was going to wear the bikini in India. She said it was a reminder of how I reacted when I saw her in it. She would have liked to buy the blue dress also, but she wouldn't be able to hide it easily. I told her she looked absolutely lovely in the blue dress, and the same went for the bikini. The sales lady gave me a bag with all her clothes and the bikini in it. Kavita grabbed my arm as we walked out of the store. She wasn't aware she was squeezing it tightly. I discretely pulled back on her fingers, and she eased her grip. I said, "Thank you," very softly. She said, "Sorry," in a barely audible whisper.

We had been shopping most of the afternoon. We also took frequent breaks to allow Meena to rest because she was not able to take a nap, and we were rather concerned. They both decided to skip lunch so they could enjoy a lovely dinner at the Indian restaurant. Kavita and I enjoyed milkshakes while Meena had an ice cream cone. We had an early dinner, and the food was delicious. We didn't linger too long and came back to the motel. Meena said she hadn't had her nap and wanted to go to bed early. That was their last night, and they had done most of the packing. They went to their room, and Kavita came back after her mother was in bed. We went to a nearby bar.

She asked me rather apprehensively, "You will be coming back to India, won't you?"

"I have every intention of coming back. I can't see putting up with discrimination any longer than necessary. Then I will have to go job-hunting over there. I know your situation in life, and I don't know if I will be able to match your standard of living."

"I'm not a spoiled brat."

I was rather amused by that statement, "Kavita, I have seen you in action on the ship and some of the shore expeditions."

"Oh, I forgot about that. Also I want you to forget about that too. Have I been extravagant since I got here?"

"No, but then I haven't taken you any place where you could be extravagant. Let's see, in Fresno we only went to the food store. In San Francisco we mostly did sightseeing. We went to the Winchester Mystery House and the beach where all you could purchase were trinkets. We went to the drive-through tree, and all you could have bought were replicas of the tree."

"You mean you have been deliberately keeping me away from shopping temptations?"

"Do I need to remind you about the shopping trip earlier today?"

She was quite defensive because she couldn't deny the facts. I could see she was having a lot of fun perusing through all those stores, and I could tell she was struggling with this subject. "Alright, what are you driving at? What are you trying to tell me?"

"Kavita, I'm aware of your situation and also mine. It is a very difficult place we find ourselves. I don't want you to be unhappy under any circumstances, and that I'll be fine with whatever you decide"

"You will be happy about it?"

"No, Kavita, I didn't say that. You should know me better than that."

"Yes I do, and I'm sorry. I know what you are talking about, and I just don't want to talk about it."

"We have to talk, otherwise recriminations would be dire, and it could be a major problem for all concerned."

"What do you mean all concerned?"

"Kavita, your parents will be affected, and they might blame me for your unhappiness. The only thing I ask is please don't be like you were during the last few months."

She was quite surprised by my last statement, "How do you know about the last few months?"

"I had a talk with your mother. I was very worried about you, and I wanted to know what was going on."

"How did you know?"

"Your letters told me a lot about your situation. You wrote sporadically, and at times it seemed like your heart was not in it."

"You understood all that from my letters? So you knew how I was feeling and what I was going through?"

"I had a pretty good idea. That was another reason to keep writing to you and pull you out of your slump."

"So you grilled my mother?"

"I didn't grill your mother. We were talking, and she volunteered the information because she was very concerned about you and was afraid of losing you because you might do something drastic. I won't make you promise, but please assure me you will not be like you were during the last few months."

"I'll do better than that. I'll promise I won't be like I was during the last year."

"Kavita, promise is a very strong word, and I won't hold you to that. Just do the best you can."

"Alright. Now tell me what do you want from me?"

"I want you for myself and myself alone. I can see you are a very loving and charming young woman. Most of all I want you to be happy because I want the best for you. I can't bear to think of you being unhappy. It was really hard hearing your mother talk about your moping."

"You will do whatever is necessary to make me happy?"

"I'll do whatever is within my power to make you happy because I don't have the world at my disposal. As a matter of fact at the moment I just have that car at my disposal, which will not take you very far. So I can't say I'll take you far and wide."

"Yes, again your knack to lighten things up. I can't be upset with you for bringing up such a heavy subject. This has been working its way up in my mind, but I have been ignoring it. I'm glad you brought this up and given us both something to think about."

It was a very emotional moment, and we were both very depressed as we fought back tears. Here was another good-bye, and it brought back memories of our parting in Genoa, Italy. It was very difficult to be positive, although we put on a brave front for each other. We proceeded to make promises we both knew we couldn't possibly keep. It didn't matter because we were resigned to accepting whatever the future held in store and we had little control over it. It was a rude awakening, and the high hopes of the yesterdays lay in ruins at our feet. We were reduced to being dejected spectators as far as our future was concerned.

We walked back with our arms around each other. I was trying to guide her toward her room, but she was edging us toward my door. She had me in a bear hug, and she was strong. I talked to her in whispers and asked her to let go of me. Finally she relaxed her grip, gave me a very long good night kiss, and went in. I entered my room and sat down to make notes, because I needed to cool off after the smoldering kisses and the wrestling. A short time later the door quietly opened, and Kavita walked in wearing a robe. I looked at her questioningly and wondered how she was able to unlock my door. She had a key in her hand, which she put down on the desk next to my key. I looked back and forth at her and the key.

"I got the key from the front desk earlier."

She had a very mischievous look on her face, and I was quite apprehensive. I couldn't make a scene because that might wake up Meena. I asked, "What are you doing here?"

Very coyly she replied, "Thought you might like some company."

"You should be sleeping. You have a big day ahead tomorrow."

"I know all about tomorrow. This is our last night together, and I want to make the most of it."

I said apprehensively, "What if your mother wakes up and finds you missing? This is the first place she'll look."

"She won't wake up."

"What makes you so sure?"

She was smiling broadly with that same mischievous look. "I gave her sleeping pills, and she won't wake up until morning."

"That was a wicked thing to do!"

"Not really. She wanted two pills so she will be well rested for tomorrow's flight."

"I still say it was wicked."

"I don't know what you mean!"

"With comments like that I know you are up to no good."

"Did you enjoy seeing me in the clothing store?"

"I enjoy seeing you anywhere and everywhere."

She persisted, "I mean all those clothes I was trying on?"

"Any particular one you want to know about?"

She sat on my lap and kissed me passionately. "Yes, the last pieces of clothing I tried on."

"You mean the pieces of clothing you almost had on?"

"Yes that one—well, actually two pieces."

"I thought you looked wonderful in those two pieces."

"You didn't say you enjoyed seeing me in those two pieces."

"Kavita you know very well I enjoyed seeing you in those two pieces of clothing."

"Then why were you ordering me to put my clothes on?"

"I was afraid of your mother seeing you. Like I said, she would have accused me of corrupting her daughter. As if I could corrupt her daughter! I'm afraid her daughter might be corrupting me!"

"So the only reason you were telling me to put my clothes on was you were afraid my mother would see me and blame you?"

"Yes, mostly."

"Well my mother won't be coming around tonight. So you don't have to worry about her getting upset with you."

"What would she get upset with me about now?"

"The same reason you thought she might get upset with you in the store."

"You mean about the bikini?"

"Yes. I mean this."

She got up and dropped her robe. She was wearing the bikini.

"She took two sleeping pills and is fast asleep. She won't be getting upset with you."

"Kavita, don't do this."

"What are you talking about? I haven't done anything."

She pulled me up and locked me in a bear hug. I was afraid to touch her and kept my arms down. She was not happy and told me to hold her. Reluctantly I put my arms around her, and I felt her sensuous bare skin. She was kissing me, and I couldn't help getting aroused. She looked at me, laughed and pressed harder against me.

"Please stop."

She was not listening. I was trembling and so was she. I hadn't even thought about picking up any condoms because I knew we would have no opportunity with her mother being around. I was sure she wouldn't be far behind if Kavita came into my room. How was I to know she would take two sleeping pills!

"Kavita, you shouldn't because this is dangerous territory. Please stop and go back to your bed."

It was a withering protest. She was not paying heed and pressed her lips on mine to keep me from talking. I couldn't push her away because she had her arms locked around me. She pushed me, and I fell backward onto the bed. She straddled me, and we kissed for a while. After a while we sat up and she gave me a big hug and a kiss that spoke volumes.

"I'm not sure how long it'll be before we see each other again. It's akin to our kissing since I got here, and now I really kick myself for not kissing you on the ship. That would have been wonderful and would have sustained me through those dark times after I got back to India. How will I feel if I let this opportunity pass me by? Besides, I know how I should be and what I should or shouldn't be doing. I've been good and proper all my life, and I'll have to be good and proper for the rest of my life. Can't I be a little bad right now?"

"Since you put it that way, how can I deny you? I'm very sure your kisses on the ship would have gone a long way to keep my spirits up. I was also kicking myself for not kissing you. Here is what I was thinking later: 'Why didn't I kiss her? I had a feeling she wanted to be kissed. I should have thrown caution to the wind and gone for it. What's the worst thing that could have happened? I'm sure she wouldn't have dumped me. A woman who had me fondle her breasts and naked behind…. Oh my, I should have kissed her.'"

She said, "So both of us wanted to kiss, yet it didn't happen because our upbringing and culture held us both back."

"Besides you were very bad today, or have you forgotten?"

"Yes, I was bad today! I loved seeing you squirm, which really aroused me and whetted my appetite, sending sensuous energy coursing through my body."

"You know this could lead to a huge problem."

"Not really. My married girlfriend gave me these."

She pulled a couple of condoms out of her bikini top. I was not happy she let me carry on the way I did, but then she wouldn't be Kavita if she had followed all the norms. She was snickering as she waved them in my face while I was fixated by what she had in her hand and wondered how it was she had brought them all the way from India.

She asked, "Why didn't you think of getting condoms?"

"Right! My thought was your mother wouldn't have been far behind if you came into my room."

"Well, she won't be doing that tonight! I want you, and I want you now!"

She straddled me after pushing me back onto the bed, and started to unbutton my shirt. I fumbled and got her bikini top unhooked. She tossed it upward, and her voluptuous breasts made their appearance with the tits staring straight at me, daring me to touch them. I was like a deer caught in headlights, but the challenge was not to be passed up. I caressed and fondled her soft breasts. She was frustrated the buttons on

141

my shirt weren't unfastening quickly enough. She yanked both sides of it, sending the remaining buttons flying. She removed it and bent over to kiss me. I took my hands off her breasts to hug her, which pushed them against my bare chest setting it on fire.

I saw the desire and determination in her eyes. 'What Kavita wants Kavita gets' came to mind because she was not the type to take no for an answer. Slowly I pulled myself out of my daze and focused on her. She was tugging at my pants to take them off, but I hadn't noticed much after her top went flying exposing her gorgeous breasts. I arched up so she could remove my pants. I removed her bikini bottom, pulled her down and kissed her while pushing my shorts off. We held each other tightly while our naked bodies undulated with passion and desire. She was on top kissing me while I massaged her breasts, and my body smoldered with excitement.

She handed me a condom, and I put it on. She lay next to me and pulled me on top. She guided me in, but let out a small scream as I entered. I froze and asked if she was okay. She answered by putting both her hands on my behind and pulling me down hard. I entered more deeply into an unknown place as my body tingled with pleasure. I was concerned because she seemed to be in pain, and she encouraged me by a prolonged kiss. I lifted myself on my arms and hands and was fascinated with her breasts bouncing around. She put her hands on them, but I pulled them off telling her I loved to see them dance. I put my hand on a breast to massage it, and she put her hand on mine to encourage me. All through that she had a wonderful smile on her face.

I felt uncontrollable energy shoot through me as I climaxed, and she shuddered with pleasure. The sexual sparks exploded, and I collapsed on top of her. I pushed myself up on my elbows to keep most of my weight off her, but she pulled me down because she wanted full body contact. I started to roll off, but she tried to keep me from doing that. I told her it was not a good idea because I didn't want the condom coming loose. I came back to the bed after washing up and we had a wonderful session of hugs and kisses. She told me her girlfriend had warned her sex might be painful, but it was nothing like that, and she really enjoyed it.

I looked at her and said, "So you came prepared with condoms. That is so wicked!"

"Yes. I come prepared, but not in the way you are thinking. I came prepared in case you couldn't control yourself."

"Well, it was more the case of you couldn't control yourself. I would never have guessed there was a raving maniac inside you waiting to be unleashed."

She was not happy about that remark, "Raving maniac? Well, maybe a little. All those sips of beer I had out of your glass must have something to do with it, but mainly it was the bikini. I saw how you looked at me and how you couldn't take your eyes off me, yet you were so miserable. Were you really concerned about my mother seeing me or was it that you couldn't touch me?"

"I had a feeling you wanted to wrestle me to the floor right there, just like you wrestled me to the bed here. I can't believe how strong you are."

"I'm sure I couldn't have wrestled you to bed if you were using your full strength because you are bigger and stronger than me. Yes, I was teasing you. The sales lady told me I had you in the palm of my hand, and I could have knocked you over with a feather. Or just blown on you and you would have fallen over."

"She probably was right. You were a heavenly sight, and I'm glad I have a lot of pictures of that moment."

I walked her back to her room, but she was loath to go to her bed. Even in the subdued light I could see her pleading eyes asking me to let her stay with me. I had to push her through the door because I didn't want her mother waking and finding her missing. I kept the door open a crack to see her quietly tiptoe to bed. I went back to bed, and it didn't take long for me to fall asleep while dreaming of our wonderful lovemaking.

I was in the between state of sleep and wakefulness, basking in the afterglow of physical intimacy with Kavita, a voluptuous, sensuous woman. I felt someone climb into bed with me. Then I felt a naked body next to me, and I felt breasts against my back. I smiled to myself, 'What a lovely dream, reliving the previous night's wonderful experience.' I never had a dream this explicit. In my dream I was going to turn around to face the woman in my bed, but was jarred to full wakefulness by a hand stroking my belly and chest.

"Kavita?"

"Yes, my dear. Were you expecting someone else?"

I felt a bit mischievous and replied, "Yes, but you will do!"

"Oh, you! I don't know why I put up with you."

I turned on the light. It was four in the morning.

"What a wonderful way to be woken up. I'm sure it is every man's fantasy."

"Thank you. I was ready to leave after your smart remark."

I held her very tight, "Please don't go. I was half asleep when I said that."

"Okay, I forgive you. You better be good from here on."

"I'll do my best. What if your mother wakes up?"

"The alarm didn't wake her. We'll wake her in a couple of hours."

"And in the mean time?"

She replied by straddling me and kissing me tenderly. She removed my jockey shorts and began exploring my nakedness. We were locked in a tight embrace with lips glued to each other. My whole body shuddered from her breasts pushing against my chest. We fondled each other, and our bodies intertwined in a lingering sensuous hug. My entire body was flushed with excitement, and I assumed she felt the same. I nibbled at her neck and slid down to her breast. My mouth found the nipple, and I felt it grow taut with excitement. Kavita stiffened and pushed my face hard against her breast. She found my shaft and pumped it up to its full glory with her gentle stroking. She was pleased with her accomplishment. I moved my hand to her crotch and massaged it. I put my finger inside her at the same time she put her hand around my shaft. The sexual act of a few hours earlier was swimming around in my head as I looked forward to enjoying being inside her again. We both trembled and shuddered as we fondled each other.

I thought about the previous night, and it was as if in one fell swoop I learned all I needed to know. The disconnected, bumbling, unknowing and all-round buffoon was nowhere to be seen. It was quite a switch from the earlier encounter when I was tentative about everything.

She handed me the condom and watched me put it on. "Did I do it right? Do you approve?"

She sat up and examined it. She saw some bubbles on one side and tried to remove them, but they only moved to the other side. Impatiently she tried a couple more times only to lie back down as if to say, 'I give up. Get on with it.' She pulled me on top, and I kissed her as she guided me in. She let out a small squeal—of joy this time, not pain as before. She pulled me down harder onto her breasts. I pulled myself up on my hands to see her reaction and also her breasts doing their sensuous dance. I grabbed one of them to fondle it, and Kavita put her hand on top of mine to guide me. She was doing something different, and it took me a few seconds to realize she was moving her pelvis rhythmically to match my movement. It helped me penetrate deeper and increase my pleasure. It was also very nice seeing the wide smile on her face. She kissed me with passion I didn't know she had.

144

All too soon I climaxed and collapsed on top of her. She kept moving her hips for a while. She tightened her arms around me and held me there. I asked her to let go—again not wanting the condom to come loose. She shuddered and slowly loosened her grip. I lay next to her to catch my breath after rolling off her. She reached down to play with my member. She moved her hand up and down like she had done earlier, but I told her to be gentle as it was too sensitive right after sex. She fondled me gently, but wouldn't let go. She also had a leg over mine to keep me from getting up. In the meantime my arousal was fading despite her fondling. Pretty soon the condom came off in her hand, spilling the semen on my crotch and belly. She opened them to look at the empty condom in her hand and then my crotch. She was playing in the pool of semen, and she couldn't believe how slippery it was. I told her to keep that hand away from her crotch. She sat up to take a closer look and was fascinated.

I went to clean up and take a shower. I looked at her as she came into the bathroom to wash up. Soon she entered the shower and we proceeded to soap each other while rubbing our bodies together. She rubbed her foamy breasts against my front and back. She soaped my member and was toying with it. I was already partially aroused and slowly it was fully erect. Expectantly she gave me a pleading look. I wanted sex as much as she did, but we were not doing anything without a condom. She pouted, but understood.

I pushed her back to take a closer look at her breasts. She put her hands under them and lifted them up toward me. Playfully she asked me if they were my favorite. "Of course!" was my immediate reply and bent down to nibble at one. She cooed, pushing my face harder onto her breast. I felt her shudder and throw her head backward. I switched breasts and she did the same. Her nipples felt so good in my mouth. We turned round and round in the shower to keep us warm while she continued playing with my member. She hugged me and it slipped in. I was in a panic and tried to pull back out, but she had me in a bear hug, and I couldn't move. She looked at me with a bright smile and at the same time I felt pressure on my member from two sides. I breathed a sigh of relief—it was between her thighs, and she thought I had done that deliberately. I didn't want to spoil it for her by telling her it was an accident. She started stroking back and forth while keeping her thighs squeezed. That was quite a turn on, and I joined in. I climaxed, and she held on to me tightly. We kissed, and I pulled back to look at her. She had tears in her eyes, but was smiling broadly. I kept my member away from her crotch by kneeling before pulling back out. We washed up thoroughly, came out of the shower and toweled each other dry. We took our time doing that because it was so very sensuous.

It was time for her to wake her mother. I watched longingly as her voluptuous body got covered up by the robe, and she walked out of the room. It was still dark as I watched her slip into her room. With a deep sigh I started getting dressed to take them to the airport. Later I knocked on their door, and Kavita opened it a crack. I told them to knock on my door when they were ready.

We arrived at the coffee shop and placed our orders. We were sitting there looking glum, and Meena gave us an understanding nod. We acknowledged that and squeezed each other's hand under the table. Actually Kavita squeezed my hand rather hard. I looked at her, and she gave me a mischievous smile while pushing my hand up her skirt. Luckily there was a tablecloth obscuring her actions. I gave her a stern look and tried to pull my hand back, but she held on tight. I massaged her thigh and she pushed my hand further up her skirt, and I played around in there. Breakfast arrived, and I pulled my hand out to go wash up. I came back and she was almost finished eating. Evidently she had wolfed the breakfast down. She unzipped me, and proceeded to play with my member.

We finished breakfast and headed to the airport. Kavita was being her mischievous self and massaging my crotch. She threw her shawl on our laps, and put my hand between her legs. I was uncomfortable doing that and pulled it out, but she put it back and pushed it further up her skirt. She unzipped me and put her hand inside. Earlier she had insisted I not wear my jockey shorts. I was wondering why at the time, but now I understood. I had no choice except to play along while she massaged my member. She had asked me to take the long way to the airport. We arrived at the parking garage, and I pulled my hand out. Meena got out of the car and was out of sight. I reached inside Kavita's top to pinch her tit. She was surprised, smiled at me and whispered, "I love it!"

I located a cart, loaded the luggage and we went in, Check in was a breeze, and we were walking to the waiting area, but Kavita was moving as if her feet were made of lead. I put my arm around her waist and nudged her along. We sat down and Meena gave Kavita a package, which she handed to me. I looked at her quizzically, and she said, "Just open it. It's a little something from us." It was a lovely off-white sweater. I put it on after taking my jacket off, and it fit perfectly. Kavita said it looked wonderful on me. I thanked them and said I would wear it all the time to remind me of the wonderful time we had together. I asked how they got the size right. Meena had sent a sales lady over to discreetly look at the size of my sweater I had hung on the rack where Kavita was trying on clothes. I vaguely remembered a sales lady next to me while we were going back and forth about the bikini.

Meena nodded at us, and we went to a deserted waiting area nearby. We sat down in a corner facing a wall. We held hands and talked about minor generalities. She would give me sly looks and would giggle. She had her shawl over the front of us, and we fondled each other amid kisses. Finally we had to get serious about the looming departure. We embraced with her face on my shoulder. I could feel her tears and hear her muffled sobbing. I did my best to console her, but there was not much I could do, and my tears fell on her shoulder. She pulled back and we wiped each other's eyes. All too soon the flight was called, and we came back to Meena. I touched her knees and thanked her for coming and bringing Kavita.[6] She was moved and gave me the blessings of long and prosperous life. Kavita saw how that gesture affected her mom. She was going to bend over and touch my knees, but I stopped her and gave her a hug.

She was confused. "Why can't I touch your knees? You touched Mom's knees."

"It is generally for the older generation."

Meena said, "Although a wife can touch a husband's knees."

It was extremely hard watching her leave. They both turned and waved before they went on board, and I stood there transfixed. My eyes were filled with tears, and my heart was in my throat. After a while I sat down and watched the plane pull away. I saw it take off, and gave Kavita a good-bye wave before heading back to my car. The drive back was very long, and I had to stop several times to compose myself because Kavita was all I could think of. I worked very hard to concentrate on my driving. I thought about the wonderful time we had together, which helped, especially the bikini and the sexual encounters.

She telephoned from Chicago to let me know they had arrived safely. It was a brief call, and we were both having trouble talking. Still we were loath to get off the telephone. We were very happy to see each other again—no matter how brief the visit.

I was very happy to receive letters she had posted from London and Istanbul. She called me after she returned to India, and it was

---

[6]   Touching someone's knees is a sign of respect. Younger generation touches the knees of the elders, not vice versa.

wonderful to hear her voice. She had not received the letter I had posted two days after her departure. She didn't mind the airplane journey this time because writing in her journal occupied her. She wanted to capture our wonderful reunion and her trip. She had read some of my journal entries and had found them very fascinating.

A few days later a telephone call at two in the morning startled me. Groggily I picked up the receiver and heard Kavita's voice. Although the hour was late I didn't mind the call. She called to tell me how much she enjoyed reading my letter. I told her how wonderful it was having her here and asked her to thank Meena for bringing her. I knew the trip was hard on her.

A few days later I received a letter from Kavita. Her response to my letter was wonderful. She included excerpts of her new journal. She had written about her last night with me. Meena had asked Kavita for two sleeping pills so she would be well rested for the flight in the morning. She needed a good night's sleep before her trip back to Chicago.

She wrote:

I was really turned on by our wrestling match at the door to my room and feeling your arousal. I also remembered feeling your arousal on the ship and the bikini store. That turned me on even more if that was possible. I put a robe over the bikini and came to your door. It took some time for me to work up the courage to open it using the key I had obtained from the front desk earlier.

I went through mixed emotions when I came back to bed after our sexual encounter. I would cry one minute, and had to stifle my urge to break out laughing the next. I crossed my arms in front of me pretending I was holding you tight with you still inside me. Heavenly! What happened that night and the following morning was magical. I really enjoyed it, and I'm not sorry about any of that. Beer and the bikini were definitely to blame.

On my return to India I saw my married friend, Kiran and thanked her for giving me the condoms. She also had a lot of questions and I was embarrassed answering them.

She said, "I understand, and your blushing and stammering tells me a lot. I'm happy I could be helpful, and I'm so jealous of what you have. I wish I had someone like Rajinder before I was married. I used to daydream about a distant cousin I had my eyes on. I visited him a couple of times and tried to get his attention. Unfortunately he was absolutely oblivious, and I would come away disappointed."

She continued, "Come on, you can give me some idea about what happened. You must have used both condoms."

I nodded and gave her a big smile.

"Seems to me you wished you had more."

I nodded.

"Okay, give me details. Don't leave me hanging like this! Don't forget, I'm the one who gave you those condoms."

I was very embarrassed, but slowly and haltingly I related the incidents. "We were on the deck of the ship, and a gust of wind blew my skirt up high exposing my behind to him. I wondered if he thought I was an exhibitionist. Later on we embraced, and I felt his arousal. I was very turned on and put his hands on my butt. It didn't take long for him to slide my skirt up to grab my naked butt."

"He did that? And you let him? Is that when you did it?"

"Yes, he did, and yes, I let him because I was the one leading him on. There was no place available for us on the ship. Later in California we had a bikini encounter at a store. You don't know anything about a bikini. I'll show you what it looks like."

Kiran was fascinated, but was not sure what that could entail. I changed into the bikini and showed her. She looked at me and wondered why I had forgotten the rest of my clothes.

"No, this is what women wear on the beach."

She was flabbergasted. "Then what happened?"

I told her about your reaction, how you couldn't take your eyes off me. She couldn't believe I let you see me in it, and she was almost breathless.

She said, "You thanked me for the condoms. Did he throw you on a bed and had his way with you?"

"Actually I threw him on the bed."

"You threw him onto the bed? You?"

I explained about sipping beer out of your glass and the after-effects of the bikini encounter.

"Later that night I went into his room and surprised him. I was wearing the bikini under my robe."

Kiran got more and more wide-eyed. "Just the bikini?"

"Yes. He knew what I was up to and tried to talk me out of it, but I wouldn't listen, and we had a wrestling match. I knew he was not using his full strength when I threw him on the bed and straddled him."

"You had to convince him? Now that's a switch."

"That's true. He didn't want me to do something I would regret. That was our last night together, and I didn't want to waste it. Soon we were smooching and had our clothes off—actually his clothes off because I was wearing just the bikini. He put one of your condoms on, and we made love. The entry was slightly painful, but the experience was heavenly. Another thing I really enjoyed was his comment about my breasts. He said he loved seeing them dancing."

"You mean you had the light on? Were you watching him?"

"No, I had my eyes closed. Evidently he had his eyes open. The light was on when I walked in, and we were busy to think of turning it off. For me that was a huge turn on because he was admiring my breasts and enjoying seeing them dance."

"If that was your last night, how and when did the second condom get used?"

I looked at her intently, "There was the following morning."

She was even more wide-eyed, "Morning? You said you were leaving in the morning."

"Yes, I woke at four and went to his room. That was when the second condom was used, and it was even better than the previous night. Later we showered together and I wished I had another condom."

"You mean he was ready again?"

"Yes, we did it in the shower."

"You did it in the shower? You were in the shower together? How did that happen?"

"After we made love he went to the bathroom to clean up. I went in to wash up as soon as I heard the shower come on. He looked at me from the shower and gave me that come hither look. Actually I was already in the process of getting in with him.

"We were fondling each other and were both very aroused. I wanted sex again, but he wouldn't without a condom, and I was disappointed. He slid it between my thighs and we continued. It was not the same, but I enjoyed it very much. I had to have him—if not inside me, then between my thighs was just fine."

She sat there shaking her head, "Unbelievable. Is he a man or a machine? I'm so turned on right now I would grab any man walking by."

"He is a man, all man. A machine wouldn't be considerate of my feelings. I feel the same about grabbing a man, but wouldn't grab any man walking by, only Rajinder."

Kiran looked at me intently. "Keep him away from me. If I get near him I will not be responsible for my actions. You understand?"
With all my love,
Kavita.

I looked at the last comment from Kiran. I was sure Kavita was thinking, 'Right. You will have to go through me to get to him. Good luck with that!'

I was touched by what she wrote. She telephoned before I could write to her. She said, "That was quite an experience we had shopping."

I replied, "Yes, you looked wonderful in that blue dress and the bikini."

"It was the bikini's doing. I saw how you looked at me, and how you couldn't take your eyes off me! Yet you were so miserable. Were you really concerned my mother would see me or was it the fact you couldn't touch me?"

"A little of both, I guess. You were relentless!"

"You have a point! I was teasing you!"

"You were a wonderful sight. Little did I know you were setting me up for your coming charging into my room and throwing me onto my bed! I guess finesse is not your strong suit! I'm glad I have pictures of that moment in the store."

"I refuse to answer because I don't want to incriminate myself!"

I said, "Your comments in your letter about our last night together really tugged my heartstrings. You were a tigress unleashed, and I was lucky to have escaped unscathed. I didn't think you had that in you."

"Oh yes, blame me for getting excited—as if you had nothing to do with it!"

"What did I do?"

"Making me put on the bikini for starters."

"Making you put it on? In other words I ripped your clothes off and forced the bikini on you. Does that make any sense? The ripping your clothes off part I can understand, but at that point what sane man would force anything back on you?"

"Mmmm. Interesting thought! Why didn't I come up with that? I should have had you in the dressing room with me."

"I should have bribed the saleslady, and she might have let me in there with you. She stretched the rules by allowing me in the women's dressing area anyway. Besides, all I was doing was standing around while you were trying on dresses."

She said, "Oh yes, and conveniently standing near a table with bikinis on it."

"I …."

"You did say you were wondering how I would look in one."

"That was not telling you to put it on."

"Go ahead split hairs. At the same time were you also thinking about the girl in a bikini at the beach?"

"What girl on what beach?"

"Rajinder, at the rate you are forgetting things it won't be long before I won't be a distant memory."

"Fat chance. Don't even talk like that. Yes, I was thinking about some of that. Don't blame a guy for that. Haven't you looked at a man and had some wild thoughts about him?"

"That is quite an admission. And no, I never had any such thoughts about a man."

I said, "Now who is not telling the truth?"

"I forgot to add 'ever since I got to know you!'"

"Nicely done, Kavita. I'll admit to looking at the girl in a bikini and wondering how you would look in one. I never thought I'd actually see you in it."

"That's better, and it led to something wonderful. I will always cherish that night and the following morning."

"Kavita, so will I!"

Chapter 6

Year Two

Review of the previous year.

It has been quite an eventful year, and a very trying one because there was no parental supervision of any kind. All my decisions had to be reached without any their guidance. Back at home there was the overwhelming confidence that their protective hand was always there, and I could always fall back on them for support at my time of need. In one sense I have been lucky because I haven't been struck by any serious illness except for the cold I had some days back. I have been extremely busy, and I just didn't have time to feel lonely or homesick.

(My recent note on this: I had heard, 'Kids leave home to set the world on fire, but keep coming back for more matches.' Well, going home for more matches option was not available to me!)

The worst of it was the discrimination I experienced in Reedly, Dinuba and other surrounding towns. It was very disheartening when I was looking for a job and an apartment. I had never experienced anything like that, and it was a huge eye-opener. Here it is the great United States where all men are 'created equal'. This is in the constitution—the master document and the protector of all rights. This is quite a cruel joke, and I will use a phrase I heard from the Americans themselves, 'It's not worth the paper it's printed on.'

It's funny how my hopes and aspirations changed over the previous few months. Here are some of my thoughts after I arrived in California:

"I have landed a temporary job and have high hopes of getting a permanent one soon.

"In this short period I am earning ten dollars per day, but I'm not satisfied and am on the lookout for a better paying job

"I've found a steady job. I will be making fifteen dollars daily, but I am still not happy. I will stick to it for a couple of days to get the knack of the job, and then I am going to start a new job hunt. I will carry on until I have the job I want."

It didn't take long for me to learn I better be satisfied with the job I had. This was not the case of jobs being scarce, but it was a case of my not being acceptable for the job. Luckily I was a fast learner, got the message, and changed my tune. "I'm not happy with the job", changed to "being glad just having a job." Reality has its way of pounding you on the head. Sometimes that is what it takes to understand the facts of life here. My friends and I have had that point driven into our thick skulls over and over again.

I came here to study, and all of this has been quite an education. This reminded me about an incident in my high school in Delhi in the mid-fifties. Our chemistry teacher told us several Americans were at our school talking to teachers about going to America for training. After his interview we asked him how it went and if he was going to America. He said they were not happy with him. They asked why he wanted to go to America. He had replied it would be a nice learning experience and maybe he could teach the Americans a thing or two. Essentially their answer was, "What the hell do you Indians have to teach us Americans?" Well Americans, maybe he could have taught you how to treat another human being with dignity, decency and respect. Maybe he could have taught you how not to judge a person strictly by appearance. That also brings to mind an incident about a year after my arrival here. I went to a very interesting party with a woman I had met. It was nice meeting youngsters my age and we had nice interaction. The main thing I remember was the problem they were having with the ice-cream maker. They had been turning it for over half an hour and it had not frozen. I stuck my finger in the water/ice on the outside of the ice-cream maker and realized it was not cold enough. I poured a handful of salt in there and took over turning the handle. They were flabbergasted and objected to my putting that much salt in the outside container. In short order the ice cream was ready. I had been making ice cream in India and realized more salt was needed to lower the temperature of ice/water mixture. Here was one Indian who taught the Americans something!

In India I was as different from the majority of the population as I am here. We Sikhs are only two percent of the Indian population. Never did anyone look at me like I was looked at by the Americans. My friends and I were talking about this situation, and we Indians weren't the only ones being discriminated against. Others included Polish, Irish, Japanese, Chinese and those with darker skin color—the list went on and on. It is pretty much part of the history of the United States, and what the

Mexicans and other minorities went through really hit home. I'm sure that is why the Mexicans were so empathetic to my plight.

The constitution did nothing to keep the Africans from being enslaved. Someone said some Americans thought Africans were not people, and we had a good laugh. One student said we could have been in a lot worse situation. They could have rounded us up and put us in camps. He had read that happened to the Japanese during World War II.

Job discrimination was not the only thing we ran into in Reedly, Dinuba and neighboring towns. Looking for an apartment was equally challenging, and I was greeted with the same rant: "Sorry, it has just been rented."

It has been a year of uncertainties, the fading of certain images, then the forming of new ones and an almost lost hope of the future. One thing is for sure. I've come to know Americans and how they feel about us. This also has been a year of brand new experiences. This is the first time I've earned money. Farm work is available all year round, and it is easy to keep a part-time job. Of course, it won't be steady, and it will have to be in one place and then another. Here I'm doing farm work, something my ancestors have done since time immemorial. I only hope I will be able to get a good job to save money and fulfill my purpose here. Right now everything is shaky and undecided. I'm like a drowning man clutching at straws trying to find something to keep me afloat. After all, you can't be too sure about anything.

Recently I came across a letter I wrote to Daddy. I had forgotten about it and had given it up as lost. I think it is worth recording here:

My dear Daddy,

I received your letter the other day. I'm sorry I couldn't reply earlier because I was really busy. When I say busy, I really mean 'busy.' These days I'm fighting a pitched battle trying to keep afloat.

Right now I have a job of driving a Caterpillar tractor from six in the evening to six in the morning. You got that right—all night! The job seems steady, but far from pleasant. There is the slow grinding motion of the tractor pulling the plow, the darkness of the night and the knowledge there isn't anyone around within two miles. I get on the tractor and keep on tugging at the proper lever to keep it going straight. The big part of the job is staying awake. There is dust, noise and the constant rattling. Night temperature falls below freezing, and that is a bit of a pinch.

Here is my typical day. Just arbitrarily I will let the 'day' start at seven in the morning. I take a quick shower and have breakfast while glancing through the books. At nine I report to college. After classes I hurry back, have lunch and at one in the afternoon I go to bed. I am up at 4:45, drive to the job and drive the tractor from six in the evening to six in the morning. I head back and start all over again at seven.

How do you like it? A stinker, isn't it? With determination I have adapted to this routine from the first day I took the job. I can say with certainty I'm fresher in the morning than all the other students. The latest development should dispel any remaining doubt in your mind about the car being a basic necessity. Right now it is my provider, and I just couldn't have thought of getting this job otherwise.

I forget where and how I came to write this letter. It would have been madness sending it to Daddy and it wouldn't have done him any good. My schedule was a killer, but I kept it up for a few weeks. Unfortunately the rear wheel bearing on my car gave out. Luckily I hooked up with a really nice repair shop. He hauled the car in, replaced the rear end, and he only charged me fifty dollars. I needed the break, and that was almost more than I could afford. He had it back on the road for me in two days, and I had to walk the five miles to college. One day someone gave me a ride, which saved me walking half the distance. I lost the job because I couldn't get there.

Other than that things have been quiet. I posted a letter to Daddy recently, and I hope to receive a reply in a few weeks. I wrote to Mom a few days before that.

Last night I had a weird dream, and I only remember part of it. I was on a slippery slope, sort of a hillside, and I was trying hard to make my way up to the top. I would carefully move one foot up, followed by the other and repeat the process. I would slide part way down and then start back up. I finally managed to make it all the way to the top without falling, and had a feeling of great satisfaction as I looked down on the world below. I felt I really had achieved something by this climb, but I'm at a loss about the significance of this dream. Could it be I'll make it unscathed to the top? Only time will tell, and I hope and pray that would be the case.

A big part of this year was Kavita. She had called from Chicago to let me know they had arrived safely. It was a brief call, and we were both having trouble talking. Still we were loath to get off the telephone. We were very happy to see each other again—no matter how short the visit. She has been a wonderful support and made the year bearable, because life would have been much harder without her. She was a lost soul for a few months after getting back to India when her grandmother passed away, and I did what I could to keep her spirits up. She said my writing about my grandfather's passing away really helped her a lot. It pushed her to do some writing herself, which helped ease her pain. I was seventeen when I wrote about Grandfather, which blew her mind and challenged her to be more creative. I kept writing to her even though she was sporadic in her replies. Often it's the small things that help.

Seeing her and holding her made it all worthwhile. She traveled halfway round the world to see me. Hat's off to her parents—especially her daddy—for doing that for her, and indirectly for me. My thinking was: 'What did I do to deserve her?'

That was swirling in my mind as I stood there at the San Francisco Airport awaiting her arrival. I had been going through pretty hard times myself. It all fell away the moment I saw her face, her bounding over to me and locking me in her trademark bear hug. My doubts and feelings had me thinking I was going to wake up, find myself in my bed and it was time for me to go to my twelve-hour all-night job. All those things happened in fairy tales where a princess kisses a frog and it turns into a handsome prince. All I can say is she made me feel like a prince for being near me, holding me and kissing me. The fact she went far beyond that during the last night and the following morning boggled my mind. All through that I was pinching myself to make sure I was awake and not wandering around in fantasy land—something I was prone to do often. What a woman!

Her departure left a huge void, but that is life and those things happen day-after-day. I tried to remember the wonderful things that happened over the previous year and looked forward to more of the same. I'm an unabashed optimist—sure beats sitting in a corner waiting for the sky to fall. There have been countless predictions of that happening since time immemorial, and luckily it hasn't fallen yet—notwithstanding Chicken Little.

Kavita and I had been corresponding rather sporadically. I would write to her every couple of weeks even if I didn't hear from her. It would be a short note to let her know I was thinking of her and asked her to write to me. I had wonderful intentions of writing every couple of weeks, whether there was a response from her or not. That soon fell by the wayside, but I kept track of my letters on the calendar to make sure I wasn't too lax in writing. She was always apologetic about being late in replying. She didn't have much to say—most of the time it was variations of, *I miss you and wish you were here.* This was very hard on me, and I really felt for her. I did my best to keep her spirits up because I was really worried she might fall into a depression. I would let her know about college and how hard I had to work at various jobs. A letter from her would be cause for celebration because it was a wonderful sign she hadn't forgotten me.

I tried hard to pull myself together because I just didn't have the time to mope. I pushed myself harder to keep busy and stay focused on my studies. It didn't help because Kavita kept popping into my mind, which would bring a pained look to my face. I did my best to work around it because I had to carry on. In time it got easier, but there was no escaping her. So I shifted tactics. Whenever she came to mind I would think of wonderful times we had together. I would think of our first embrace, her arriving in California, our two weeks together, our last night and the following morning, and . . . . I had plenty of those episodes to relive. It didn't stop her from popping into my mind, but it reduced the pain because I concentrated on the happier times.

Is Kavita a woman I'm not destined to be with? Is she destined to be just a fond memory? Will we see each other again? How would I live without her? A love like ours just couldn't just die.

Epilogue

I had sent Daddy advance copies of the letters and the journal, before I had put it all together into a book form. He had not yet studied all I sent him because the family would grab those letters. I'm sure he would go through them more thoroughly and get a more profound picture of my life here during those trying days. I also warned him about the fact that what was in my letters to him was not the same as what was in my journal. He told me he understood, and it will be interesting reading. What he read in my journal absolutely blew him away, and he wrote me the following letter. Something like this from a parent is what all children crave and live for. It needs no introduction or explanation.

Letter from Daddy

My dear Rajinder,   September 15, 2009

I have gone through your letters and journal. At this time it was a cursory read only, but what shook me most was the agony and struggle you went through during your early days there. I admire your will power and strength of character to bear it alone. I do realize you didn't want to be a burden on the family, but what good are parents if they cannot help their son in his hour of dire need?

Your luck of good health played its part, for without that one cannot work for eighteen to twenty hours a day. This consisted of studies and manual work at odd hours of the day and night. To tell you the truth I, for one, may not have been able to bear it, although I also have gone through my own hard times. Your account of living day-to-day with hardly anything in your pocket is harrowing. The worst part is that we didn't have an inkling of the troubles you were going through. I'm really proud of your will power and power of resistance for facing the ordeal on your own.

It also proves the often-repeated proverb: 'all that glitters is not gold'. People assume once they cross over to America it would be an easy life with lots of dollars in hand, not realizing one has to earn a livelihood in all sorts of conditions.

I'm also surprised to read some of my own letters to you, some of which I seem to be quite philosophical. For example, my letter dated twenty-fifth of August about your account of the car journey to California. Even now it sends shudders through my spine when I imagine my son drove a distance of 2,700 miles alone in four days in an old vehicle that also stood the journey marvelously well.

We are all praise for the struggle you went through in the early part of your life. The best part is that you didn't give in during those moments of adversity.

Yours affectionately,
Daddy.

There was nothing unusual about saving letters I received from Daddy, although saving them for five decades is. Keeping copies of letters I wrote to Daddy was quite fortuitous for a nineteen-year-old.

I was going through some storage boxes when I came across a box marked Letters, and at the bottom of the box was an old folder from my first two years in America. I had carefully filed the letters from Daddy and copies of my replies to him. Interspersed were letters I exchanged with Mom and my brother, Ravi. What an extremely pleasant surprise! Later I found the journal I kept during that same period. They had been buried for five decades.

I started transcribing those letters for Mom, Daddy, my children and grandchildren. I felt they might enjoy revisiting my life as a nineteen-year-old. My close friend, Jacqueline was fascinated by what she read and suggested others would like to read about my adventurous journey to America half way around the world, and my loving relationship I had with Daddy. I was not too convinced, but I went ahead and started putting it together. I had sent a draft copy of all the transcribed letters to Daddy. He was very fascinated with what he read about my life fifty years earlier. In the meantime my journal had been transcribed, and I sent him a copy. I warned him what I was writing in my letters and what was in the journal were two different things. He concurred and said it would be very enlightening. What he read in my journal really blew his mind. Of course, he had some idea about my trials and tribulations, but nothing prepared him for what he read. After reading the journals he wrote a letter to me dated September 15, 2009.

Jacqueline prodded me, and she has been a driving force behind the writing of this book. Once I got going it was an all-consuming project. Jacqueline has read through it multiple times for typos and also recommended changes and improvements.

What Jacqueline suggested felt right. We have been working together intensely to bring *California Dreamin'* to life. She felt the book was lacking in emotional depth and made good suggestions on what the reader would like to know about my life. Multitudes of revisions, corrections and additions have morphed into this story about my first two years in America.

The writing of *California Dreamin'* has touched me profoundly. I have finally realized how courageous I had to be to leave the comfort of home knowing I wouldn't see my parents or brother for five years. This book hits home how important my family really is.

I was wondering if Jacqueline would question the part where I wrote about discrimination. She didn't even raise an eyebrow because she was born of Japanese parents in an internment camp in Colorado. She saw her father being discriminated against as she was growing up, and she had been subjected to discrimination herself.

I have enjoyed sharing my experience through creative writing. I am an engineer, and there was absolutely no way I could have imagined myself being a writer. Want an example of an *oxymoron*? An engineer who can write would be a perfect one. All you have to do is try reading through some of the instruction manuals written by engineers. This part does not reflect just my thinking on the subject. The following quote is from a clipping I saw either in the sixties or seventies:

"4 yeres ago I culd not spell Unginere. Now I r one."

Note about my being at the boarding school for five years starting at age of seven. It was a wonderful experience and I'm glad I was there during those formative years. The only problem was there was not much hands-on experience. I'm glad Daddy pulled me out of there when he did because that was instrumental in my becoming a well-rounded individual. If I had graduated from the boarding school then I would have been more of a book-worm without any hands-on experience. I wouldn't have done any radio building, nor would I have built a transmitter, record player, or oven. That also meant I wouldn't have been as handy as I am now.

Telephone call From Kavita

A few years had passed. One day I was sitting at my desk at the office, and the telephone rang. "Hello, this is Rajinder."

There was no response and I said, "Hello, anyone...."

"Hello Rajinder, this is Kavita."

I had trouble hearing that because it was barely above a whisper. I was jarred by the name, but something was not right about the call. The joy of hearing that name was short lived when I realized the call was not from India, and I didn't recognize the voice either.

"Look, Kavita is in India. This is not an overseas call."

She was sobbing, "Please listen to me. This is Kavita."

"No, you are not. Who is this?"

There was a pause on the line and I heard her struggling to talk. Finally she spoke in a very low voice, "Rajinder, please listen to me. This is Roshni."

That was barely a whisper, and I would have missed it if I hadn't been listening carefully. That hit me hard and sent me reeling.

"Kavita! How wonderful to hear from you! Are you all right? Where are you?"

"I....... I...... think I am......:" she could barely speak.

"Please speak up. I can barely hear you."

She said sobbingly, "I'll call you when I can talk. I.... love..... you."

With that she hung up. Those three little words grabbed me by the throat and swung me around. I had tears in my eyes, and I sat there shocked and perplexed. Why was she crying? She needs my help, but where was she? How would I find her?

I should have kept her on the phone longer. I didn't recognize her voice because she was whispering and crying. I hoped she'd call again.

More in my sequel: *Kavita, My Beloved.*

GRANDFATHER

He passed away in 1960. He is the one I wrote about.

Author Bio

My father was born to an illiterate farmer in a tiny village in Punjab, India. His father knew the importance of education and did his best to educate him. He, in turn, passed on these values to my brother, Ravi and me.

I was attending a one-room school in the village. The teacher retired, and the school closed because no replacement was available. I was then enrolled in a school in a neighboring village. Daddy was concerned I was not getting a proper education. He found a boarding school, and at age seven I was enrolled there. I received an excellent education at the boarding school. The best part was my English teacher, Mr. Kashyp who was a teacher par excellence. Later I had him as my English teacher again at the high school I attended in Delhi. He was a short man with a very commanding presence. He was a hard taskmaster, a very strict disciplinarian with a dry sense of humor. He was fair and took wonderful care of all the pupils in his charge. He was also the housemaster of my boarding house in addition to his teaching duties. He had touched a lot of lives and he had a major hand in shaping me into what I am today.

Daddy was a junior officer in the Indian Army, and he got the worst postings. These were non-family stations, and we couldn't be with him. Finally Daddy was transferred to Delhi, which was his first posting at a family station. He pulled me out of the boarding school so we could be together as a family. The high school I attended in Delhi was an excellent educational institution, but its outward appearance was very deceiving. The whole school was under tents, and there were no buildings of any kind. That meant no heating in the winter and no air conditioning in summer. Despite that there were several hundred students enrolled there. I attended the school for three years and received my Senior Cambridge high school diploma.

Interesting how life experiences prepare us for challenges down the road. My early stay in America would have been much more challenging without the experience of living at the boarding school.

I arrived in this country in early sixties with enough money for a couple of quarters at the college in Indiana. I was pretty much on my own here and had to scratch out a living by the skin of my teeth. Being in a foreign country was quite hard. Major part of my early stay here was the discrimination I faced in California's Central Valley. It was eye-opening experience and had me wondering if I had done the right thing coming to this country. There were fleeting thoughts of packing up and heading home, but my financial reality made that impossible. I made the best of it and pressed on. I really appreciated help from the Mexican co-workers and Mr. Miyamoto of the Farm Labor Office who really looked out for me and did his best to have weekend jobs lined up for me. Also I have to make a special mention of Nikos, the Greek foreman who hired me. He knew what I was going through because he had been a foreign student himself. I'm sure it would have been a lot harder for me without their support. In San Jose I got help from the manager of the Manpower office.

That brought to mind my reading about the problems faced by immigrants from India in early nineteen hundreds. They were really up against impossible odds because of Immigration Acts of 1917 and 1924 that pretty much banned Asians entry to America and put a stop to Indian immigration. The primary reason was to curb Chinese immigration. After that the Supreme Court declared Indians were not white and couldn't become citizens. (That despite the fact Indians are classified as Aryans, which means we are not a minority!) That also meant they were aliens and couldn't own property, which forced them to sell their houses and businesses. Most of them were activists against the British in India, and were escaping their tyranny. They had renounced Indian/British citizenship and couldn't reapply. They couldn't go back to India because they would be arrested, which meant they were basically stuck in limbo.

I read about a family that came from India and worked very hard to assimilate into the society. The father wore dapper American suits and was a very successful businessman. He bought a house and was well established. The immigration act caused the bottom fall out of his American life, and he had to sell his house and close his business. He was distraught because there was no way to climb out of that huge hole he found himself in and ended up committing suicide. He came to America for a safe haven, but ended up as a classic case of, 'Out of the frying pan, into the fire.' Knowing American history of British oppression, one might think Americans might have been empathetic to the Indians' plight. One might be wrong! They were relegated to the underclass status. What would you do if you couldn't find any kind of employment and there were no sympathetic people like the Greek foreman, Nikos to take a chance on you? Of course, I didn't know about this during my early years in India. It just goes to show what all immigrants could be facing and have to bumble through the best they could. I wonder what all could be in store of some other minorities in this

166

country. That really gave me a huge pause after reading what my countrymen went through at the time and my experiences in the sixties paled in comparison.

Of course, people from India were not the only ones caught up in that dragnet. The primary target was the Chinese, and I'm sure they were no better off. Then there was the case of the Japanese being incarcerated during the Second World War. Current (2017) developments are mirroring the events of early last century where immigrants from various countries are being bashed and declared persona non grata. Goes along the saying—more things change, more they stay the same!!

Finally I had to bow to the inevitable and changed my appearance so I wouldn't stand out like a sore thumb the moment I stepped out of the apartment. It was a huge load off because availability of jobs improved some, and I didn't get all those funny looks. Shortly after that I moved to San Jose, California, and it was as if I had landed on a different planet. Jobs were not really plentiful, but I was getting jobs that were unavailable to me in the Fresno area. I also connected with the Manager of the Manpower office. They provided temporary workers to various businesses in the area. It was the classic case of first come, first served, and I was getting pretty good at being the first one there. That allowed me to have the pick of the available jobs. Also there were times when no jobs were available, and I would wait around the office hoping for a call to come in. That gave me a chance to talk to Terry. He got to know my qualifications and that I had a B. S. degree with a background in Electronics.

One day I was on a job unloading a boxcar of lumber with another worker. Later in the day I saw Terry come into the warehouse, and we both wondered if he had received a complaint about our performance. He talked to the foreman who came over to tell me Terry wanted to talk to me. Apprehensively I walked over there and was sure I was going to be fired. Terry was very cordial and had further questions about my education and experience. He saw my quizzical look and told me Memorex had requested a technician and I was the only one with qualifications that came close to what they wanted. I was quite excited about that and he told me to report to Herb at eight Monday morning. Terry said I was not to wear my grubs because I would be working in the Quality Assurance Lab. I was absolutely blown away at that turn of events and thanked him profusely. He said I was the one who needed to be thanked because he wouldn't have been able to fill the requisition otherwise. That was really funny—a job coming to me on the proverbial silver platter instead of my running all over carnation looking for one! Sure was a huge boost to my confidence and made me realize I was not quite as useless as I was led to believe in the California's Central Valley.

I thought it was just another temporary Manpower job, but this turned out to be a life changing event although I didn't realize that at the time. Thirty days later Memorex hired me from Manpower because they liked my work ethic and my expertise in magnetic recording. At the time the company manufactured computer and instrumentation tapes. Later they filed a petition for permanent residency on my behalf. (The letter they wrote to Immigration Department is included in Epilogue.) That turned into a career that spanned almost three decades. That sure made up for all the badgering I endured in the Central Valley, California. The best part is the pension check they send me every month like clockwork.

At Memorex it was nice to be judged on what I could do, not what I looked like. All the technicians in the department were foreigners. One was from Canada (Russ), one from Japan (Tach) and one (me) from India. The boss was an American, and his boss was from England. In those days Memorex made computer tapes, and I took courses to brush up in the magnetic recording field. The work was quite exciting for me, and I enjoyed myself because there were no discrimination problems. You did your job, and you were rewarded accordingly. I was progressing professionally, and Memorex had accepted my B. S. degree from India. My writing skills were very handy, and I was getting important assignments requiring writing of final reports. At times I got my name on the report simply because I wrote it for the engineer, and he was only too happy to acknowledge me because he didn't have to go through the hassle of writing it.

The 1953 Oldsmobile I drove to California was on its last legs, and I was sad at having to get rid of it because it had taken such good care of me. I drove it to a junkyard and was waiting for it to open. A man approached and asked what I wanted. I told him I was there to dispose of the car, and he asked me how much I wanted for it. I said, "Make me an offer." He offered ten dollars. I put my hand out, and he put a ten-dollar bill in it. I handed him the keys and signed the title over to him.

Memorex was going downhill after the top management decided to get into the mainframe computer business. That was in direct competition with IBM, but Memorex didn't have the resources for the venture, and ended up closing the operation down. Layoffs were common and I was looking at my options. My friend, Pete was working at Fairchild, and he had me come in for an interview. They made me an offer, which I accepted, and I had a very interesting couple of years there. I was working on the Optical Character Recognition chip, which was the precursor to the digital cameras we have these days. Unfortunately, the oil embargo hit about that time, and I was caught in the third round of layoffs. That was the time PhDs were working as gas jockeys because jobs were scarce. I went into business for myself to tide me over and that lasted for five years. By that time the economy was humming, and I was losing workers to the industry left and right. I was just a training ground for the industry. I decided to put an end to that and sent out resumes. Memorex called me in for an interview and made me an offer, which I accepted. I was glad to be back with the old company, and they were glad to have a former employee back. The best part was I would have ten-year seniority after one year and be fully vested in all the benefits, including the pension.

That took me back to earlier days at Memorex. I was running the Q. A. laboratory in the Consumer Audio Department of Memorex. The problem was they couldn't produce a decent tape and were always behind the competition in various performance characteristics. (That was pretty much par for the course. At the time they were also trying to come up with a 1 Megs Byte hard disk without any luck.) My boss (and I presume it came from his boss) was pushing me to make our tapes look better than they were so they could be shipped. I was not too sure about that, but I was feeling the heat. So I fudged the tests to meet their criteria and the various batches that were on hold were allowed to be shipped. Of course it hit the fan and I was the one to be blamed because the competitive results did not hold up. I was reprimanded and that went into my personnel file. I was not very happy about that and made a big fuss. The big boss got wind of that and surplused my position, and I was told to find another job within the company. I checked around and there was a very nice job in the computer/instrumentation tapes section of the plant. I would be reporting to Gomez, who I knew from my early days at Memorex. He asked me about the reprimand in my personnel file and I explained what happened. He was going to make fuss with the big boss, but I told him it might not be such good idea.

Gomez hired me, and I worked hard to make sure he was happy with my work and didn't have any regrets. A few months later he came to my office and put my personnel file folder on my desk. I looked at him quizzically. He told me I was free to go through it and discard anything and everything in there I didn't like. He also asked me to add any positive reviews in there and he would sign that boss' name to it. He was sure the person would have no way to object. I did a major cleaning and also put in a glowing review from the previous department head—precisely the man who had screwed me. My boss forged his signature, and signed what all I had put in. He sent the folder back to personnel department. The sanitized file folder was what they saw when I applied for the job. No wonder they had no questions for me because they thought I was golden and they better grab me before I took another job!

I was given a cook's tour of my work environment. The senior engineer showed me the Engineering Computer Lab (ECL for short) where I would be working. He was pointing out the computers and various pieces of ancillary equipment. I just nodded as if I understood, but I had not seen any of that up close. Two years later the manager of the ECL quit. I decided to pursue the job and landed it. Here I was now the manager of the Center! This was the crucial nerve center of the engineering research and development of Memorex products, which was a huge plus for me. I learned a lot on this job, and it really broadened my horizons.

Later the ECL was taken over by the Data Processing Department. They were used to running a stable computer center. The ECL was anything but that because it was in a constant state of flux. This was the nerve center of Engineering, and the various departments were testing the disk drives, controllers and other ancillary devices that attached to the IBM computers. Engineering was developing and testing the next generation of those products, and ECL's only reason for existence was to support this effort. The configurations and software had to be constantly updated to accommodate Engineering's requirements. This was something very novel to Stevie, the head of the Data Center where changes were to be avoided like a plague. They didn't understand the extremely fluid nature of the ECL where system configurations were changing constantly. They needed to be proactive in anticipating the needs of the various groups and make sure the required software, hardware and computer systems were in place when they were needed. This included IBM's newest mainframe computers and other support equipment. This was to assure our equipment was compatible with the newest and greatest computer systems from IBM. There had been cases where the customer had purchased the newest mainframe computer from IBM, and attaching our drives to that computer had caused the system to crash. You stand there with egg all over your face because the drive had not been tested with the new IBM computer system.

The new people charged to run the ECL were from the Data Processing center. It was a power grab with nary a thought to the understanding of what they were getting into. They had Engineering people jump through hoops thus slowing down the process of making changes and upgrades. I had been reassigned to a new department in the Data Processing section. The people from Engineering were complaining to me about things not getting done and asked me to take back the ECL. I told them I was powerless to do anything, and they would have to take it up with the heads of the department, David and Steve. That resulted in the projects were not getting completed on time. Those louts didn't understand the basic reason for the existence of the ECL. It was treated like a stepchild and starved for resources. The Peter Principle had triumphed yet again!

Here is a rather hilarious example of their ineptitude. We were in a meeting with George, the head of my department. One of the engineers, Atul was getting ready to go to Singapore on company business, and he asked the manager about the visa. He was a young software engineer from India and would need a visa to get into Singapore. I immediately knew what he was talking about, but the manager looked at the young engineer blankly, and I decided to have fun. I waved my Master Card at him and told him it was a very good alternative. Atul was puzzled by my reaction because he figured I, of all people present, should know he was talking about the entry visa for Singapore. He saw the smirk on my face and realized I was just having fun. He waved his American Express card at me and said it trumped my Master Card, but it wouldn't get him into Singapore. The manager finally realized what the engineer was talking about. He was from the inner clique of Data Center management personnel, which epitomized their level of incompetence. What was going on in the ECL was probably going on in the Data Center at a much grander scale.

There was going to be a major downsizing of Unisys, and they were discussing plant closings all over the country. The top Management in Blue Bell, Pennsylvania was not happy about goings on at Memorex. Based on the above I can fully understand why Santa Clara, California plant ended up on the chopping block.

My friend, Jacqueline, encouraged me to fill in the gaps in *California Dreamin'*. Jacqueline is also writing her own book, 'Three Part Harmony—Learning, Healing and Moving On'. It is about her healing from three episodes of breast cancer, the death of her second husband and moving on with her life.

Short note about my friend, Maldev. He died in a car accident.

MOM

DADDY

Appendix

Copy of the Letter Memorex wrote to Immigration Department:

March 13, 1967

District Director
Immigration and Naturalization Service
630 Sansome Street
San Francisco, California

Dear Sir:

It is my understanding from Mr. Rajinder Singh and his manager, Mr. Finn Jorgensen, that Mr. Singh and Memorex have been delinquent in communicating with your organization. Speaking for Memorex, I must apologize for not having answered your letter of October 31, 1966, asking for information as to the status and whereabouts of Mr. Singh. Due to shifting responsibilities in the Personnel Department, this letter was never brought to my attention. Therefore, I would like to describe at this late date the several reasons why we at Memorex are so interested in keeping Mr. Singh on the payroll.

Since 1964 Mr. Singh has worked as a Research Engineer, current salary $673 per month, and has been in charge of various projects, some of which pertain directly to NASA and other agencies. Much of the recording of the moon shot, Mars fly-by and manned satellite recording has been done with Memorex instrumentation and video tape.

Relatively speaking, our company is rather small and the skills and knowledge for research and manufacture of magnetic tape are exceedingly difficult to find. Mr. Singh's work in research involves the exhaustive check-out of our tapes; the design and development of special tape transports; and the establishment of standards and specifications according to NASA and the Bureau of Ships' requirements to be used by Quality Control.

In the one-year period that Mr. Singh was engaged in this work, he completed the following studies:

    Shim Wear Test Evaluation (for the Lockheed contract)
    Hot Calender Experiment (for a new type of tape)
    Durability Test
    Coating Resistance
    New Oxide IRN 135

He has also established a Revised Tape Library Cataloguing System. He has recently completed several other studies, among which was an analysis of all standard tapes and an abrasiveness study.

He now operates a very complex tape department, the equipment alone exceeding a value of $100,000, and he has contributed ingenious approaches to involved and complicated procedures which have resulted in improvements in our research programs.

Mr. Singh's future at Memorex as a professional researcher leaves no doubt as to his economic independence and technical growth. He has proven himself to be a dependable, creative and very loyal employee. The number of his salary reviews is above average and aside from the present immediate problem, we can see no reason why he should not continue to progress in a manner that would increase his interest and technical creative skills.

We would certainly be pleased to have his case reopened for consideration. We would like to consider Mr. Singh a permanent employee in our Santa Clara research organization.

Very truly yours,

E. J. Shannahan
Manager - Industrial Relations

CTB246   WW BUA016 GOVT PD BU ASHINGTON DC 29 224P EST

MR RAJINDER KHOKHAR

2092 SULLIVAN AVE SAN JOSE CALIF

INFORMED BY IMMIGRATION SERVICE THAT YOU WILL BE GRANTED AN
ADJUSTMENT OF STATUS ON JANUARY 2. CONGRATULATIONS AND BEST
WISHES.

DON EDWARDS MC

Telegram from my Congressman, Don Edwards about my getting the
Green Card. December 1967.

1956 War over Suez Canal

Egypt had nationalized the Canal. In my opinion the major reason for the war was the prevalent racism and the British couldn't envision Egyptians being able to run it. According to them the Egyptian revolutionaries were a rag tag group of people and General Neguib was the front man. The real power behind him was Colonel Gamel Nasser who was the visionary and his first target was the continued British military presence in the Suez Canal. That was also the opinion of all Egyptians. The other part was the British feeling it was a global power and could run roughshod over the upstart countries like Egypt. Their empire spanned the globe although their prized possession, India had slipped their grasp. They also had the feeling they were responsible to protect the populace from the tyrannies of the Communists and others of that ilk. Countries all over the world were feeling more and more nationalistic and they wanted their freedom. Those countries had to be pushed back and shown who was in charge. On top of that those countries were being patronized by the Russians while Americans were coming around as the self-appointed leader of the free world.

In this case it was America that came to Egypt's rescue. Allen Dulles, the American Secretary of State had okayed the British/French/Israeli adventure without checking with President Eisenhower. The trio went on war path and started bombing and strafing. Eisenhower saw that and he was furious. He had the matter brought up in the United Nations and got a ceasefire resolution passed. That brought the hostilities to a screeching halt and withdrawal was initiated.

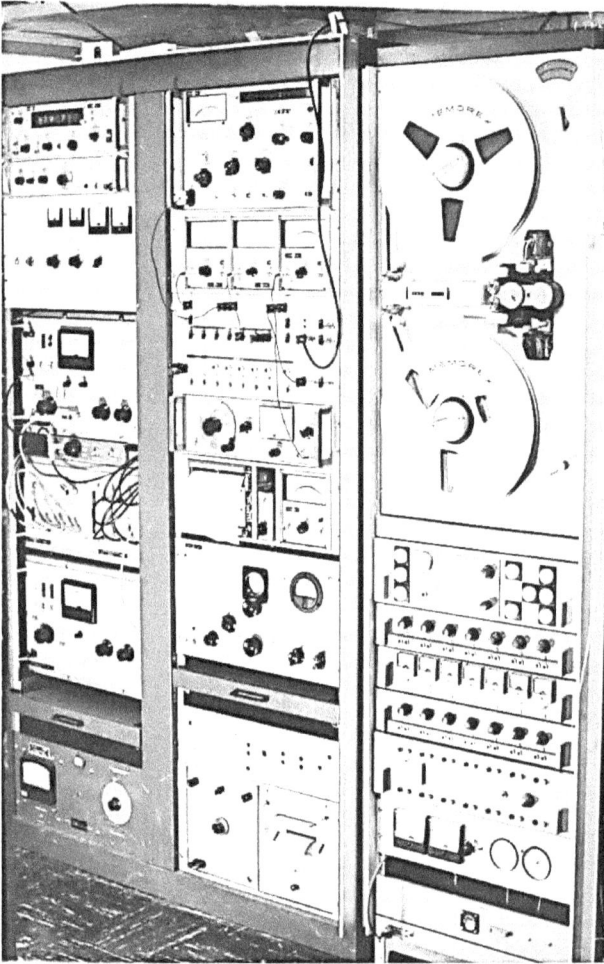

Figure 1. Research FL-1100 station

Above is part of the $100,000 equipment that is mentioned in the letter to Immigration Department. In contrast I would like to mention I had bought a three-bedroom, two-bath house at the time for $15,000. That same house currently sells for over half a million dollars. In other words, the equipment value would currently be $3,333,333!

Letters

Letter from Daddy
Received in Egypt

December 11

My dear Rajinder,

I hope you had a comfortable journey up to Port Said, and you are enjoying the voyage. I wanted to write to you at your Aden stop, but I thought I might be cutting it too close, and the letter might not reach you in time.

I arrived back at my place at seven in the evening after your ship's departure. It was an enjoyable short trip.

I'm sure you noticed I was a bit quiet and morose while others were having fun throwing flowers and garlands to the passengers on board the ship. That was to be expected because a member of our small family was leaving for four to five years. That was bound to put me in rather a depressed mood, and I felt a bit down. I hope you didn't mind.

What is the ship's routine? Did you go ashore at Karachi and Aden? Who are your cabin-mates? Did you play any indoor games? How was the weather on board? How was the food?

Yours affectionately,

Daddy

Letter to Daddy, January 18

My dear Daddy,

I don't remember what all I wrote in my last letter since I didn't keep a copy. I'm confident I gave you all the details of my arrival and the arrangements made for my stay. I have been going to college for two weeks. Teaching here seems strange after what I experienced in India. You can sit with legs stretched in front of you or placed on an adjacent chair.

Everything is going along pretty smoothly. Living seems to be much cheaper here compared to Indian standards. Ranjit and I are trying to live frugally, and we do our own cooking at all odd hours because it is much cheaper than eating in the cafeteria. The only problem is we can't get whole-wheat flour. Otherwise we get all the necessities, even curry powder especially made to impart Indian taste. The way of making purchases is also very novel. Here we go into the store and use a cart to pick up all we need. The prices are stamped on the articles, and it makes the process very easy. The cashier totals them up and gives us the bill. You know exactly what you are buying.

So that is what is going on. More when I hear from you.

Yours affectionately,
Rajinder

(My later note: In India we would give the shopkeeper our list and all that would be collected and bagged for us. They also had delivery available.)

Letter from Daddy, January 23

My dear Rajinder,

I had seen your letter of the first of January, and I had written a page to be enclosed with your mom's letter. I hope you have received that by now.

What have you finally decided about the branch of your studies? Have you switched to Electrical Engineering? I read in one of the brochures your college has the arrangements for teaching electronics. What are your plans of changing the institution? Your roommate must have completed his first quarter by now. Has he found a part-time job?

How is the weather? Did you need to purchase any additional clothing in America? Did you buy a watch in Aden or after reaching there? How do you like the college?

The countryside here is absolutely drab and barren these days. The greenery will return at the end of March. Till then the whole area is gray interposed with white patches of snow, and the big lake is also frozen in the mornings.

Yours affectionately,
Daddy

Letter to Daddy, January 27

My dear Daddy,

My last letter was not a very long one, and I couldn't tell you much about this place. I have been here a month, and I can give you a better picture of my feelings and reactions. The college keeps me very busy because I've taken eighteen units. Some days it is just two hours of classes and on Tuesdays I have six hours. The professors are very nice as are the students. All the professors are easily approachable, even the Dean of the College.

It is a very nice town, and the people seem hospitable. Yesterday we celebrated the Republic Day of India with great pomp, and there was a good crowd to see the variety show we presented. People were very pleased with the program, and it was a great success. The forty students of the India Association worked hard on the show. Fort Wayne has three radio stations, three television stations, and supermarkets galore. You can see even a relatively small town has all these.

Otherwise everything is proceeding smoothly. There are no shops open on Sunday, and it is a bit of a challenge if we miss shopping on Saturday.

The weather is very cold, and the temperature falls to seventeen below. Walking is rather treacherous, and I have had two bad falls already.

It is shocking news about Marina's father passing away. I have written her a letter of condolence.

We are trying to keep everything reasonable. We walk about a mile for groceries. There is a small shop a hundred yards from us, but it is more expensive than the big store.

Everything is moving along fine, and the overall stay is really enjoyable. More when I hear back from you.

Yours affectionately,

Rajinder

Letter to Daddy, February 12

My dear Daddy,

This is terrible news about Marina's father passing away. I was very worried about her when she didn't show in London. I was almost sure she had been in a car accident because she was a maniac behind the wheel. I wrote to her from London before I knew of her father's passing. I've since written her a letter of condolence.

I haven't received a letter from Mom for some time. I wonder what's up with her. Other than that I've received a letter from my old classmate, Vijay and my cousin, Daljit. That's about all the correspondence I have besides you. I'll write at least once to everyone, and then let it go at that. I will reply to the letters as they arrive. I've written to the village to fulfill my promise to Grandma.

I've already switched to Electrical Engineering. I haven't been able to get a job yet, but I've done some lawn mowing and other odd jobs. Something is better than nothing. I've not found it necessary to purchase any additional clothes because the ones I have are sufficient. I thought I had already written to you about purchasing a watch in Aden. I paid six British Pounds for it, which comes to about sixty-seven Rupees. It is a good calendar watch and keeps perfect time.

Being in the Sikh uniform (turban and full beard) is fine with me. There are times some other Indians don't like it because being in this uniform gives us some sort of distinction. When Americans are talking to a person from India, I might attract their attention if I was nearby. They would turn around to say hello to me and start chatting with me. Those Indians do not openly express their feelings, but they make no secret of their displeasure. Of course not all Indians are like that, just a small number from Bombay. We try to stay away from their lot. Among the Americans we seem to be quite a curiosity.

Yours affectionately,
Rajinder

Letter from Daddy, February 17

My dear Rajinder,

My letter was delayed because I was away for ten days. I also went to our village for a day.

Your mom and Ravi are okay. They sent your parcel of traditional clothes on the twelfth. He told me the expense of airmail was almost equal to the actual cost of the items contained therein. Please try to minimize the mail expenses.

Thank you for sending your photograph. It is very nice, and I will have a copy made for your grandmother.

You have not written about the courses you have selected. What about your roommate? Has he made any plans for the change of college?

Your last letter was quite informative about the town, the climate and your day-to-day life. In fact your place is even colder than here, although the living conditions are more comfortable. Still it is always better to be a little careful about sudden exposure. I'm sure you are taking all the necessary precautions.

Ravi told me your roommate has written home about getting a job. Don't forget to write to your grandmother in the village. She was asking about you and is expecting to hear from you.

Yours affectionately,
Daddy

Letter to Daddy, February 23rd

My dear Daddy,

Your recent letter was wonderful compared to your earlier ones, which were more like questionnaires. I think future letters will be even more interesting than this one. While on the topic of letters, I've already written directly to Grandma. My correspondence diary tells me that was on the third of this month.

I received a letter from Mom in the parcel, and I've already replied to that. As regards the parcel, I was well aware it was going to cost a great deal, but I had to have it by a specified date. The Punjabi clothes were needed for the Republic Day function we were holding, and I'm glad they arrived by that date. I knew air postage is costly because I had sent some articles by air to Marina. I'll be more careful and try not to put any unnecessary strain on the budget. Punjabi clothes were not available here, and I had to ask Mom to send them.

While on this subject, could you order me the foreign edition of Hindustan Times? It is a weekly newspaper and will cost approximately five rupees per month.

At the present moment we have no plans to change college because it will be easier to start afresh in the fall. We have yet to pick the institution.

The other day we went to the party given by the society of the wives of the college professors. (Faculty Women's Association.) It was only for foreign students, and the professors were not invited. The President of the college was the only exception. The party was very interesting, and we enjoyed talking to all the ladies present. Mrs. Boriak was the liveliest one. She is hardly five feet tall in her high-heeled sandals and rather plump. This added up to her being the center of attention. I'm over six feet tall. She stood next to me and asked, "How tall do I look?"

After the party President Keene came over to talk to us. He shook our hands and bent over to read my name tag. He said hello and then proceeded to have a nice chat with us.

It has been snowing and it really has piled up this time. We went out for a stroll last night, my first experience with fresh snow. It feels like soft cotton, and walking on it is really tingling. I had an urge to go rolling down the slope, but thought better of it. The temperature is not as low as it has been. Still we have to be careful not to expose ourselves to the cold, and I'm fairly comfortable in my overcoat.

The first term is coming to a close, and it's nearly two months since I arrived. We are kept very busy: classes, homework, housework, cooking and cleanup. Our usual sleeping time is one in the morning, and we are up at seven to be at the college by eight.

Yours affectionately,
Rajinder

Letter from Daddy, February 23

My dear Rajinder,

I'm glad to know you have finally decided in favor of Electrical Engineering because you have a natural bent of mind for this, and I'm sure you will do very well.

I'm also happy to learn about your bargain of a watch from Aden, and I can see how much cheaper it was as compared to India.

It has given me immense pleasure to learn you Sikhs are commanding greater attention of the Americans than other Indians. I really don't know why the majority of students choose to change their identity by shaving off. I hope you will stick to the Sikh uniform. Of course at certain places you may be looked down upon, but there is nothing like maintaining one's identity and facing the odds as and when they arise.

Life here is rather quiet because there are never more than two officers here since my arrival. Your battery-powered radio is very handy, and the battery is still doing well, although the voltage seems to have gone down some.

It's good you have written to the village. This business of writing replies to everybody must be costing you quite a bit of time. Where did you get the typewriter for typing the letters? Is there any possibility of getting a typist job after your first quarter?

Yours affectionately,
Daddy

Letter to Daddy, March 7

My dear Daddy,

I know you will be surprised to find the enclosed clipping from the college newspaper, *The Nucleas*. You will see my photograph, which was taken at the party given by the Faculty Women's Association. From the photograph you will realize how short Mrs. Boriak is and how high I tower above her. I still remember how she came up next to me and asked, "How tall do I look?"

Mrs. Shaw asked us to dinner. She works at the college post office and is really a good cook. Their son, Lynne and daughter-in-law also joined us for dinner. I had told them we don't cut our hair. His comment was, "If everyone embraced your religion, I would be out of work." Lynne is a barber. We had a pleasant talk with them. We were three guests and were seated around the table so none of us sat next to each other. The conversation was quite pleasant, and they asked good questions about India. One of us was a Christian, and he talked about the spread of Christianity in India.

We clean the apartment ourselves because there are no servants available in America. Besides, we couldn't afford one anyway. Moreover, there is not as much dust and dirt as we have in India.

I have purchased a typewriter, and chances of getting a typist job are remote because they are taken by women.

Yours affectionately,
Rajinder

Letter to Daddy, March 14

My dear Daddy,

   I have something more to say about my photograph in the college newspaper. I didn't know it would be published. I'm standing there with a broad smile on my face because I really enjoyed meeting Mrs. Boriak. She is so funny, and she kept us all smiling and laughing through the evening. It had been a while since I had laughed so much. My being here is rather serious business, and I'm following the old adage, 'Nose to the grindstone.'

   The first term is coming to a close, and we are in the midst of finals. The next quarter starts on the twenty-seventh, and I have already signed up for classes. I'm again taking eighteen units because this term I will be taking electronics circuits, and I want to concentrate on that. After the next term I will need ninety-seven units for graduation. This will take six quarters no matter how many units I take. There is no use burdening myself with the extra work when the time to graduate will be the same.

   We have been keeping very busy, and at the end of this term we will have a week off. That will be the first relaxation from the tight schedule we have had all this time. We might be bored because we are so used to being exceedingly busy. I really do like this system of work here.

   More when I hear from you.

Yours affectionately,
Rajinder

Letter from Daddy, March 17

My dear Rajinder,

Your letters take roughly eight to ten days to arrive. Mine take longer because sometimes the weather is bad and there are no flights for three to four days.

I have received your newspaper clipping, and it is very nice. I can well imagine the contrast in heights. I'm really happy to know you are mixing with the people there, and they enjoy your company. Keep it up. One thing you should keep foremost in mind is the parties should not be at the cost of your education because that is the primary objective of your being there. As I say, mixing with people is also a must, and both things should be balanced accordingly.

Your account of keeping the house in order was quite interesting. It is good you are doing all the chores yourself, and it shows with the availability of facilities how much a man can do for himself. Firstly there is the pleasure one derives from achieving something, secondly, getting things done according to one's own requirements. Here we waste so much time criticizing or complaining about the work done by sweepers, servants or launderers. In fact the Indian housewife is good at criticizing the work of the servants, but not doing much herself.

Yours affectionately,
Daddy

Letter to Daddy, March 20

My dear Daddy,

Your last letter was just that—a letter, not a questionnaire. It is a wonderful transition, and I hope your future letters will be along the same lines.

It is rather funny about the Indian housewives grumbling and complaining about work done by the servants. Over here we don't have any such problems because we get our respective jobs done the best we can. It is not easy because our time is very limited. The afternoon cooking session is mine and the evening is Ranjit's. Sometimes he will lend me a hand, and at times I will do the same for him.

We are missing Indian music a great deal. We might be able to receive Indian radio stations. I am planning to get an old radio for about five dollars and get it working. If need arises I will add a tube or two. I will have the time during the upcoming break.

My first term ends tomorrow. Thanks for the subscription to the Hindustan Times, and I would also enjoy receiving some Indian magazines. I have arranged to get the Illustrated Weekly of India magazine for the next three months. I will send you Reader's Digest magazines after going through them. It will be good for you to read the American edition of this magazine.

Yours affectionately,
Rajinder

Letter from Daddy, March 26

My dear Rajinder,

Your account of preparation of food is quite interesting, and you should be a good cook by the time you graduate.

Your proposal of buying a second-hand radio and repairing it is quite sound. This way you will catch the overseas broadcast bulletins of All India Radio and be posted with the latest news from here.

I'll arrange to send you some magazines. The American edition of Reader's Digest will be very welcome, and I will be waiting for it impatiently.

The valley is now full of flowers, and all the fruit trees are abloom. In another three to four weeks this will give way to lush greenery you saw when you were here last.

How did you fare in the first term? Were there any final exams at the end of the term?

Yours affectionately,
Daddy

Letter to Daddy, March 27

My dear Daddy,

The new term starts tomorrow, so I thought I would write to you before I get tied up with studies. Also I thought you might want to hear about my recent visit with an American family. The first term results are in. I have secured a good enough position. In Math I got an A; ME a D (not very good.); Engineering Graphics a B; History a B; English a B. That adds up to a GPA of 2.94—just a hair under the 3.0 required being on the merit list.

Hope you are having good weather there. The temperature here will be going up to fifty degrees today, and we are enjoying the beginning of spring.

I have received the first copy of the Hindustan Times newspaper today. It is wonderful reading the old paper again, and I really missed it for the past three months. I will pass it on to the college library after I am finished with it. I'm sure they have never had an Indian newspaper before. It will be a while before I get the Illustrated Weekly of India. After that it will be coming weekly.

I would like to mention yesterday's visit with an American family. Mrs. Hamil looks slightly older, but I might be wrong because it's quite difficult for me to judge ages over here. They have two children, a dog and a cat. Mrs. Hamil asked her son to show me around the house. It was a nice one, about the best I've seen so far.

Then came lunch. Incidentally, for some reason they called it dinner, but I didn't care to ask why. It was a good lunch and good conversation. These Americans eat so little, and I came back almost empty-stomached. They had pickles, which Mrs. Hamil pointed out were hot. Their daughter had one bite and almost jumped from the hot taste. I said it was the normal spicy level in our food.

After lunch we had a general discussion. They wanted to see where I was from, and I showed them the city of Amritsar, Punjab on the globe. I gave them the rough history of the city and its importance to us being one of the holiest places for us Sikhs. They wanted to know about summer weather back home, and they were shocked to hear it would get over one hundred and ten degrees.

Later in the afternoon I asked for their permission to leave and for a ride home. The latter part was important, for I was well over ten miles from my place. He asked me if I had driven in this country. I told him in India we drove on the left-hand side, and I was trying hard to get that into my head so at a critical time I wouldn't turn the wrong way.

Today we had a minor celebration because this was the last day before the new term. We had curried chicken, vegetables with eggs and topped off with rice pudding. It was an enjoyable change from our normal vegetarian diet. After dinner we had a two-hour walk to settle our stomachs.

I wrote to Mom on the fourteenth, and her letter should be due by the middle of this week. I'm sure I have exhausted your patience with this long letter. Hope to hear from you soon.

Yours affectionately,
Rajinder

Letter from Daddy, April 4

My dear Rajinder,

Your letter of the twenty-seventh of March arrived today, and I also have your previous letter, but at the moment I can't find it. The house is in a disrupted state because we are packing for your mom's move to Srinagar, Kashmir. So much stuff got collected during the last four and a half years.

I'm very happy to know you have done well in the first term. Your mom and Ravi join me in sending you congratulations for the fine result. I am sure this is only the beginning, and in the next term you will do even better.

Yesterday evening your mom and I had a two-hour visit with the parents of your roommate, Ranjit. I especially enjoyed the get-together, because this was my first visit to their place.

It is getting rather hot here, and the flies and mosquitoes have made their appearance in large numbers. Last night we needed the fans to ward off the mosquitoes.

I will close this letter now because a lot of packing is pending, and I'll write to you after our arrival in Kashmir.

Yours affectionately,
Daddy

Letter to Daddy, April 11

My dear Daddy,

I am in receipt of both your letters, but I couldn't reply before this. I wasn't particularly busy, but I was slightly off mood. I didn't feel like writing with that sort of feeling hanging around. I wrote something a few days back, but I tore the letter up because I didn't like it. So here I am writing again and hope it will get through to you.

I'm very happy to receive the newspaper regularly, and I received the Illustrated Weekly of India yesterday. What a treat going through the magazine again. I will have to think of ways to keep my friends from grabbing the magazine before I'm finished with it. These things from home bring a lot of joy to our hearts. I have been able to arrange for Indian music also, and that has boosted our otherwise sagging spirits.

The other day I was talking to one of our friends. He mentioned the name Khanna and was wondering if that name was familiar to me. I asked him if the particular person was in the boarding school. He had no idea, and I was inclined to believe he was not. Later two Indian students came by. The one I did not know was staring at me all the time and trying to figure something out. He asked my first and last names. He asked me if I was in the boarding school. As soon as he said that, I blurted out his name, Khanna! You can imagine my feelings at that moment. It was a sudden burst of emotion and the joy that comes when we meet someone very dear to us.

We were friends at the boarding school, and I lost contact with him when I left the school. Imagine meeting him after eight years. It is so very difficult to narrate everything that came to mind at that moment. What a coincidence. After all those years we ended up at the same college halfway around the world. Thrilling, isn't it? We sat there chatting right up to two in the morning. He is the same old jolly self and has been out of India since he graduated. He informed me about what all he had been doing since my departure from the boarding school. He told me a few of our classmates were in America. It was wonderful for both of us meeting after all this time.

I received a letter from Mom twenty-seven days after writing to her. It is only from your side I have the major news. So it will be good if you will please kindly keep up the old spirit of writing so I don't have to complain to anyone about your being indifferent.

You have quite a point about my cooking abilities. I am wishing I better not be a good cook by the time I graduate. It is perfectly all right in my present situation, but it just won't do in the future married life. I don't feel good imagining my being in the kitchen doing everything while my wife is seated comfortably in the living room with her feet on the table and a novel in her lap while she calls out to me, 'Honey, is dinner ready?' It just won't do, and blessed are those with no knowledge of cooking!

Thanks for the congratulatory message about my results from last term. The mere fact I've done well in the last term is no guarantee I will be doing equally well in this one. The second term has started in earnest, and I have taken eighteen units this time. It will do me good as the first technical course is involved. Today we had the first test of the term. It was in math and there is no reason I should not get an A because the test was dead easy. The professor saw me sitting there and came over to ask if I needed help. He was surprised when he saw I was finished with the test and my answers were correct. The other students were still struggling with the quiz.

Right now I'm listening to Indian music, and it is a real treat to hear it again. We took the records to the landlady, and she enjoyed them. She has a very good ear for music. She is an M.D. and that is another advantage for us.

Yours affectionately,
Rajinder

Letter to Daddy, April 21

My dear Daddy,

I am doing fine and the College has been going very well. Occasionally we take time off from the tough routine to watch television. Last night we went down at nine and came back up at one in the morning. Don't worry. It is very seldom we watch television for that long, but we do save money on movies. The landlady watched television with us and has invited us for dinner tomorrow. The other day she saw us walking back from shopping and gave us a lift.

You must be having fine weather there. Over here the trees are just beginning to sprout, and the grass is showing signs of greenery, but the temperature goes below freezing at night. The days are somewhat pleasant, and today it went up to fifty-two degrees. They said they didn't expect a good summer, but you can't be too sure about this weather.

I am enjoying hanging around with Khanna. He is a very good friend and is with us almost daily. He was here yesterday, and we were reminiscing about the old times at the boarding school. We talked about the old soccer games and the basketball games. I am sure you remember the cricket match in which a ball hit me on the nose. Khanna told me about another classmate, Sib who is in California.

Yours affectionately,
Rajinder

Letter from Daddy, April 22

My dear Rajinder,

We have been waiting for your letter for the last ten days. This time the interval between two of your letters has been more than normal. I'm sure you have been extraordinarily busy during this period and therefore the delay.

We left Amritsar, and reached Srinagar, Kashmir on the tenth of April after spending one night along the way. I was rather worried about your mom because the journey was long, but we stopped along the way where we liked, and the truck had a heater that kept us warm.

We have settled in the new house. The place is small, which is good because it needs much less furniture. We brought our own sofa set, so the living room is furnished well. The bedroom is rather small, and there is just enough room for the beds. The dining room has a few folding chairs and a table. I have been staying with your mom ever since our arrival here. I will shift to my unit after Ravi gets here later this week. I asked him to look for his college admission in Chandigarh.

Yours affectionately,
Daddy

Letter from Daddy, April 28

My dear Rajinder,

It was a great relief getting your letter, as this unusually long delay was worrying us. I hope you received my letter dated the twenty-second where I wrote we were rather concerned about the delay.

No luck for Ravi on his getting accepted by National Defense Academy, and he will try once more. Next time he intends to go there after attending the preparatory course in Delhi.

I am happy to know you are getting the newspaper and the Illustrated Weekly Magazine. I can imagine your hunger for something Indian. I hope you have also received a packet of magazines I sent about a month back, and I'll send you more in a day or two.

Your account of meeting Khanna was very delightful. Now you will be in touch with more of your boarding school friends through him. Yes, the joy and pleasure one gets when meeting an old classmate is really beyond description. In this case the intimacy is free from all formalities because one knows the other, and one can talk on common matters without any hesitancy. I hope this contact with an old friend will make your stay there more enjoyable.

I'm happy to see your transcripts, and I'm sure you will not only keep it up, but will be able to improve. There should be no uncertainty about it because I'm confident you will achieve whatever you want. I am returning the transcripts as requested.

I felt an element of frustration in your letters about not receiving any replies from various people. I can well imagine your plight of waiting for a reply to your letter in a distant land where the only moments of real joy are when you hear from your near and dear ones. I'm sure your uncle Bawa wrote to you. I don't think you can expect any letter from your mom's sister because they have their own whims and moods.

Regarding the delay from your mom, I think it can only be laziness, although you have to give allowance for her brief period of ill health. You must also realize she has taken your leaving not too badly. I do see a glimmer of sadness on her face sometimes due to your absence. She has a mother's heart, and she has stood it very well. I hope I will be able to keep up the correspondence with you, although an oncoming project may also come in my way in this respect. Please try and bear the negligence of those who either don't write or write late. Don't let this spoil your peace of mind.

Yours affectionately,
Daddy

Letter to Daddy, May 2

My dear Daddy,

I just received your letter, and it was really a wonderful letter. That was rather poor news about Ravi not getting selected for NDA. Better luck next time.

As far as the delay from my side is concerned, don't worry about that. You see there are a hundred and one things I have to do that are more important. The letter can wait, but these things cannot and I hope you understand it won't be good for me if I happen to miss something because of the letters. Forget about my not feeling well and there is something wrong with me because I haven't been sick since I arrived— not even a headache.

I take your point about other people not writing to me. I think that is the way it will be, and I will have to accept it. Still, it is not very pleasant when they don't answer my letters.

It is heartening to receive encouragement from you. I am trying hard to live up to your expectations. Please don't send me anything for the next few weeks. I am not sure where I will be over the summer.

Yours affectionately,
Rajinder

Letter from Daddy, May 13

My dear Rajinder,

I'm very happy to see your results this term. I am sure you can convert the B's to A's. I will be expecting to see your name on the merit list by the end of this quarter.

This year the cold spell in the valley is rather prolonged. Normally spring rains end by April, but this time they haven't. After a day or two of sunshine we get cloudy weather again. This is keeping the temperature down otherwise it rises to nearly one hundred. The valley is coming to life, and the lush greenery is also on the increase.

I have noticed you are catching the American slang a bit too quickly. The word *damn* is appearing too often in sentences. I don't want to curb your natural expression, but I feel you should exercise a little check on this. These sorts of words do not enrich one's language and are difficult to discard. There have been a few embarrassing moments due to use of slang.

I'm still waiting for your photograph. I hope you have made friends with someone owning a camera. So far most of the people who see my photo ask if it is yours. I suggest you get yourself photographed and send us the negative for making copies.

How is your radio faring? I hope you have been able to get good reception. I don't understand how you got a B in practicals because this is your master subject. I don't mean to say B is not good, but I thought in practicals of E.E. an A was logical for you.

Yours affectionately,
Daddy

Letter to Daddy, May 16

My dear Daddy,

Last Sunday we went to a picnic party given by one of the professors, Dr. Boriak. It was for foreign students only. We had a wonderful evening, and dinner was very good. Before that there were games: badminton, basketball, football, volleyball and other activities. Afterward we went for a walk, and Mrs. Boriak showed us the places of importance including the romantic places where boys took their dates. Food was plentiful, and she gave us the leftovers to take home.

I have not been able to find any jobs. This is a small town, and there are a lot of people looking for work. I am trying my best to get out of this town in the near future. Most probably we will start at the new college in the fall. There are two possibilities—the state of Texas or the state of California. The two have their respective advantages. The Lamar State College in Texas will be good. I would graduate in two years, and the fees are low. The chances of getting a job there are better. Fresno State College in California sounds very good. The graduation there will take slightly longer, but the chances of getting a job are better. I will finally decide in favor of one or the other, and I'd like to have your opinion on the subject.

There have been more successes for me in the studies here. There have been tests in all subjects. In English I got a B and in Electrical Engineering an A. I bet you won't be able to guess the next subject—Math. I got an A and the top position in the class. All the students in this class are top performers, having a GPA of 3.5 or higher. Getting to the top of this class means more to me. I got an A in English recently, and was shocked to learn that was the only A in the class.

Yours affectionately,
Rajinder

Letter from Daddy, May 22

My dear Rajinder,

I received your letter of the second of May yesterday. The stamp on the envelope is May fourteen. I don't know where this letter has been lying around for so long. Did you forget to post it or was it perhaps lying in some corner of the local post office?

I am extremely happy to learn you are keeping good health. I know you are busy with your studies to make the grade you narrowly missed last time. You must be already preparing for the finals of the second term.

We are also quite excited about your Uncle Bawa and his family visiting us, and I hope they are able to make it. The main difficulty will be getting someone to care for his chickens. I think he might have already arranged that, and we will enjoy their two-week stay with us.

Where do you propose to go during your summer vacation? How do you intend to keep up with the letter writing? Will you be spending the two months in one place, or is it going to be an *on-the-move* vacation? What date is your vacation starting?

We are now getting fine weather here. The people started sowing paddy, and you can see the fields are full of water. The whole place looks like a virtual sea. Almonds and cherries have come to the market.

Your winter is prolonging, isn't it? What a variety of weather in this world. In places like Punjab people are getting roasted with heat, whereas you have to move around wearing an overcoat. I hope by now summer must be around the corner.

Yours affectionately,
Daddy

Letter to Daddy, May 23

My dear Daddy,

I can't understand how you can say I am picking up American slang from the one word, *damn*. I went over the last letter and couldn't find more than two mentions of that word. I wouldn't say that is too much.

You have a good point that I should have an A in the Practicals. I know the whole thing is easier said than done, and I will do what I can to push a bit harder.

Now we have the lush greenery that could be compared to what you are describing in Kashmir. The grass is getting green, and the flowers are blooming. We have a wonderful view of the landlady's flowerbeds from the window.

The radio is working really well, and the reception I get is sometimes just the same as we used to get in India. There is a good crowd almost daily to listen to India. We are so very happy to be able to listen to Indian music again, and it does lift our spirits. The reception is limited to about an hour and a half, and then it fades out. We get very good reception from an old junk radio. I did some fiddling with it and added one more tube to give it better sensitivity.

When does Uncle Bawa plan to come for a visit? He only mentioned he was planning to come over, and I'm hoping to receive a letter from him soon. Aunt Surjit promised to be quick in her letters now that I am in America.

Yours affectionately,
Rajinder

Letter from Daddy, May 27

My dear Rajinder,

I'm really delighted to hear about your further successes in the interim tests. I am sure you will not only improve on these but will achieve really good distinctions in the future.

You have written about your long driving trips to various places. Please be on the safe side of the speed limits. The roads may be very good, and you may be a very careful driver. You have to take into account others who often drive after drinking a lot. If you are driving rather slowly the chances of averting any mishaps are better. I don't mean one should just crawl along on good roads, but what I want to stress is your safety. The roads are very good over there, but proportionately the number of vehicles on the road is much higher, and speeding is the order of the day. I would like to remind you about the two major accidents that happened to your pen-pal, Marina and her daddy.

Yours affectionately,
Daddy

Letter to Daddy, June 3

My dear Daddy,

My last letter was delayed because I forgot to post it, and that is why you got it rather late.

I appreciate your comments about driving. It is Khanna's car, and he is the one doing the driving. I will pass on your advice to him.

Things are really forging ahead with the second term coming to a close. I probably won't be here after the fourteenth of June. It will be best to withhold your next letter till you hear from me. I will give you my new address as soon as I get settled. You might be surprised with vacation coming so very close I don't have a plan in place. I can't say anything about that except to shrug my shoulders and ask you to wait and see.

I believe Uncle Bawa must be with you by now. I am sure you are enjoying their visit. Oh, how I miss that place. My only consolation is I will have ample time there with all of you after finishing here.

Don't worry. I will get set up somewhere, and you will know shortly after that. Just hold your letters until you hear from me.

Yours affectionately,
Rajinder

Letter from Daddy, June 8

My dear Rajinder,

The past few letters have taken nearly two weeks to reach here. I don't know what that is due to.

I don't know where this letter will catch you. By this time your vacation must have started. I asked you to make arrangements for your mail to reach you at the new location. Perhaps you have already looked into that.

We are glad to learn your self-assembled radio is working well, and you are able to hear Indian music daily for some time. This hobby is already paying off.

I received three copies of Reader's Digest last week, and they are very good. I can see the type of advertisements appearing in American magazines. Most of the articles are also new and make good reading material. More copies will always be welcomed. By the way, did you get the first dispatch of Film Fare magazines? More are on the way.

Uncle Bawa didn't show up. We got a letter instead saying there was some hitch about getting the time off from work, and they may not be coming this season.

You asked my opinion about the change of college. I feel you should go for a good institution. I will advise you to look for a well-known and recognized college.

Yours affectionately,
Daddy

Letter to Daddy, July 7

My dear Daddy,

Now I have settled here for the summer, and you will be able to write to me at this address. There is a possibility I might move, but my friends will still be here, and they will forward your letter.

I have settled down on a job. I've been working for over two weeks, and I'm becoming quite popular. My ultimate objective is to be an all-round worker, and I should be able to take over the job of anyone. Things are moving toward that objective very smoothly.

I am keeping extremely busy. I don't have any time for writing or doing other things. Work starts at nine and continues right up to midnight. In between I have two breaks of an hour each. You realize how busy I am here, and that is the reason I've been postponing writing this letter for a week. Finally I have managed to find time to write to you, I don't have much time to spare.

Otherwise things are going along smoothly. My car is running without any problems. I had a trip to the Kings Canyon Park last Sunday. It was hilly country throughout, and the Park itself is in hills at 8,000 feet altitude. It was a very nice Park, and we saw Redwood trees. Those are huge trees with trunks wider than twenty feet in diameter, and they grow to a height of 200 feet or more. My friends and I had a lovely afternoon there.

Yours affectionately,
Rajinder

Letter from Daddy, July 19

My dear Rajinder,

I am glad to know you have settled in one place for the summer. Hearing your car is serving you well is also very heartening news. I was curious to know about the H.P. of the car and its fuel consumption. I hear petrol is very cheap over there. How much does it cost per gallon?

Your summer vacation must be half over. What date is your college opening? What are your plans for the future? Are you thinking about changing the institution? When are you expecting your results of the final exams?

You must write longer letters to your mom. Although all the letters addressed to me I read to her, I feel she expects them to be directly written to her in Punjabi. What you can do is this. Write to her and don't repeat those things to me. I imagine you will have to spend more time since you can't use the typewriter, but that should be accepted to keep up her morale.

Here we are living under tentage. The weather is just fine although it gets a bit hot during the afternoon, but the nights are just lovely. You said the weather in California is about the same as Punjab. What are the maximum temperatures? Your apartment must be air-conditioned.

Yours affectionately,
Daddy

Letter to Daddy, July 24

My dear Daddy,

I am really happy about your reaction to my purchase of the car. I couldn't have expected better, and that indicates the tremendous understanding of my thoughts and actions. It is a V8 with a horsepower of 250. It gives me about sixteen miles per gallon. It runs just fine and is very reliable. The petrol is about twenty-two cents per gallon.

I have done some traveling. The roads are good, petrol is cheap and the days are carefree. In my last letter I wrote to you about a trip to Kings Canyon Park in the mountains. Last Sunday I took a trip to San Francisco with my friends. I got to see the Golden Gate Bridge, which is a suspension bridge almost two miles long.

Recently I went to San Jose to meet Sib, another classmate from the boarding school, and he was surprised to see me after eight years. He suggested we go to Santa Cruz for a leisurely day. The road was mountainous, and we saw lots of cars pulled over because of overheating. Sib was rather skeptical about my car going over the hill considering the price I had paid for it. The car performed flawlessly, and that was a big surprise for him. We had a great time, and we visited the beaches. It was wonderful seeing all those girls in their swimsuits. I dropped him at his place and got back late.

I have decided to change to Fresno State College. It is a very good college, and I will be receiving credit for my B.S. degree from India, plus thirty units from Indiana.

Yours affectionately,

Rajinder

Letter from Daddy, July 26

My dear Rajinder,

Yesterday I received your letter enclosing the transcript from last term. I was really overwhelmed to hear about your achievement and congratulate you heartily. What else can a father expect from his son? You've found your capabilities, and I am sure you will make the best use of your talents that so far had been lying dormant.

I did need good news from some quarter yesterday. Something had gone wrong with the work site, and I was feeling miserable the whole afternoon. The mistake was made by one of my civilian contractors that affected the layout of a building, and I feared that might bring a bad name to my unit. Your letter did a lot to cheer me up. As regards to the mistake, there is nothing to worry about.

Yours affectionately,
Daddy

Letter to Daddy, August 4

My dear Daddy,

It is really heartening to receive wonderful encouragement from you. In this desolate place the only thing that keeps my spirits up is such good letters from you. The word *desolate* in the above sentence might surprise you. It isn't desolate in the literal sense but desolate in another sense. That is not just my opinion. It is the opinion of the hundreds of other foreigners who have come here for studies. They learn this first hand, and also they become painfully aware of public opinion in this country. I want you to know it all, and I will give you details sometime later.

Thanks for the congratulations, and I can really feel I have earned them. You see the whole responsibility is on my shoulders. I've gained much knowledge during these few months I've been here. It's not that I was studying that hard during the second term. As I described to you in my earlier letters I also did some roaming about. We also spent a lot of time looking after that small apartment. In other words, it's not the time spent on the books that counted, but the quality of time.

Another thing that happened was the hood of the car flew open. The damage was not huge, but it was expensive. I didn't even get a scratch.

Yours affectionately,
Rajinder

Letter from Daddy, August 11

My dear Rajinder,

I'm glad to learn you are enjoying your vacation, and your car is giving you good service.

I'm rather taken aback about your joining Fresno College that will give you a degree in such a short period of time. What I want to impress upon you is not to hurry the process of education. To my mind, this seems rather short, and I wonder if it is the right thing to do. I can only advise you, but the final decision is yours. Please think it over coolly, and don't hasten the process if the final outcome is going to be anything short of the best we want. I'll leave the rest up to you.

Does this mean you brought everything with you, and you will not have to go back to Indiana for anything? What about any documentation from the Indiana College?

We are packing all over again, and it looks to be a tremendous job because I have hardly the time to do anything, and Ravi is unavailable. One of the officers has promised to airlift the luggage to Chandigarh, Punjab. Your mom will fly there on the twentieth of August.

Yours affectionately,
Daddy

Letter from Daddy, August 25

My dear Rajinder,

     I received your letter of the eighteenth. I thought of sleeping on it and then writing a reply. Then I thought the day after being Sunday, it would delay the letter by two days, and you might not like that. In any case I'm not at all agitated or infuriated and cooling down is not necessitated.

     I must say I've really liked your frank and straightforward letters. I've read most of those to my friends, and they have admired the way you have been getting through your day-to-day life in America. You cannot expect a father who has no bent of mind toward car races to tell his son, 'Well done boy, keep it up and let us see how you fare in a blowout at a greater speed.' I do have love and affection that keeps goading me to write to you to be careful, go slow, do this and do that. This can only come from parents and from nobody else.

     I'm not trying to restrict your movements. All I wish is for you to do what you want, go where you want, but to go slower. As for my confidence in your presence of mind and your capabilities, I had no doubt earlier and have none now. This in fact is one of the reasons I didn't fill your ears with so much advice when you left for your studies. You must also know by now I'm a man of few words, and I want to say only those things that must be said. Just think if nobody shows any anxiety about one's welfare, what does one claim in this life? When you get married there will be another partner who will be able to show anxiety, but until then it is only mother and father who will bother about you and keep on bothering about you. Don't for a moment think just because I didn't say, 'Well done, boy', I didn't appreciate your coolness of mind. Something prevented me from saying that aloud, and that something is love and affection.

     I'll keep expecting these frank letters from you. Even if I seem scared after hearing any of your incidents, don't bother about it. A piece of advice from parents or well-wishers can always be taken or ignored based on the merits of each individual case. If you really feel you want us to stop offering any kind of advice, we will do so. Please tell us. After all we can't be right in all cases. Knowing full well we are not aware of the conditions over there, something in us still comes up to tell our son, be careful. I think that is the natural consequence of hearing about some incident that could have resulted in greater damage.

Your explanation for the change of college is very sound. I didn't know there are colleges that give credit for a B. S. degree from India. I really fail to understand why colleges in India don't allow such concessions, and this is beyond me. There is such a vast contrast in the systems of education. Then again, America is a land of contrasts.

Today I got your transcripts from Indiana, and again congratulate you for the fine performance. I am proud you and your brother, Ravi are both doing fine in your respective spheres.

Yours affectionately,
Daddy

Letter from Daddy, September 10

My dear Rajinder,

I never thought I was annoyed with your letter. I rather liked your frank expression of views. Anyway, my reply to that must be already in your hands. I don't want to delve into that subject any more. The only thing I want to say is keep on confiding in us your feelings of joy and excitement, including any worries. Let us all share your life in America. We might be showing little concern about certain things. It is a genuine wish about your well being. Let's continue sharing each other's views.

The weather here has started changing. By the end of this month the trees will be bare. How fast the summer season has passed. How is the weather at your end? What sort of winter do you expect in California?

You haven't mentioned if your college has started. What about the part-time job during the college days? How is the car doing? I hope you have gotten it repaired after the incident of the windshield.

About a month back you had written about the treatment you get from the local people and mentioned you would elaborate later. Will you throw some light on it now? That letter seemed to have been written in a rather depressed mood.

I have asked enough questions, and I will close now.

Yours affectionately,
Daddy

Letter to Daddy, September 28

My dear Daddy,

I received your letter a few days back. I'm sorry I was not able to reply earlier. The reason is obvious—I was busy shifting around and getting settled in Fresno. I arrived here on the fourteenth, and college started on the seventeenth. I've found an apartment about five miles from the college. The accommodations near the college are too expensive, and they were all taken by the time I arrived here. I have to be content with this place—just a roof over my head.

I see you had lots of questions in the last letter. Regarding the question about the treatment from the local people, I promise to elaborate on that soon. Also I will write about the problems I had with my roommate. Please be patient. I do not have a regular part-time job, but I've been doing odd jobs here and there.

The car is doing fine, and it is my everyday necessity. I have to make fifty-mile round trips for my weekend jobs. The weather in Fresno is quite warm, and it won't be getting any colder than Punjab in winter. Last winter it snowed here for the first time in thirty two years.

Yours affectionately,
Rajinder

EXPENSES: JANUARY TO JUNE

THIS IS IN DOLLARS.

Postage	0.70	Grocery	4.40
Paper	0.07	Postage	0.59
Grocery	2.89	Soap	0.21
Shoes	2.99	Grocery	1.53
PO box fees	0.50	Milk	0.69
Radio & parts	6.56	Grocery	2.46
Milk	0.69	Grocery	1.88
Milk	0.69	Ice cream	0.29
Postage	0.52	Ribbon	1.75
Milk	0.69	Files	0.10
Bleach	0.25	Pad and envelopes	0.50
Ivory soap	0.29	Milk	0.69
Palmolive	0.11	Stamps	3.59
Milk	1.71	Movie	0.50
Starch	0.17	Grocery	5.54
Candy	0.10	Library–Fine	0.80
Stationary	2.21	Grocery	2.62
Stationary	1.20	Postage	0.25
Drawing Instrument	17.50	Milk	0.69
Rent	5.00	Postage	0.04
Book & cover	9.08	Sugar	0.30
Transformer	4.31	Tape	0.15
Grocery	2.73	Eraser	0.15
Carbon paper	0.62	Pen	1.00
Popcorn	0.15	Grocery	4.08
Candy	0.10	Grocery	0.45
Book etc.	5.00	Milk	0.69
Typewriter	*43.80*	Linit	0.17
Brandy	0.75	Scrubber	0.05
Grocery	2.40	Rent	25.00
Books	1.00	Movie	0.50
Milk	0.98	Newspaper	0.07
Grocery	1.77	Milk	0.69
Shampoo	1.50	Grocery	4.80
Coke	0.20	Ice Cream	0.15
Radio Parts	1.57	Grocery	1.46

Coconut oil	1.95	Stationary	0.25
College Fees	250.00	Milk	0.69
R Digest	0.35	Dry cleaner	0.60
Paper	0.10	Grocery	0.98
Book, calculus	4.00	Movie	0.50
Grocery	1.05	Candy	0.10
Grocery	1.96	Bread	0.20
Postage	0.38	Letter	0.50
Postage	0.37	PO box fee	0.50
Beer	0.13	Grocery	1.23
Book racks	0.35	Candy	0.10
Movie	0.50	Grocery	5.85
Pizza	0.53	Sat Eve Post	0.20
Postage	1.18	Paper	0.25
Milk	0.69	Glass	0.15
Rent	25.00	College Fees	225.00
Grocery	5.00	Books	13.50
Eraser	0.20	Flour	0.59
Anacin	0.25	Tape recorder	19.95
Grocery	0.30	Paper	0.07
Ext Book	8.95	Eraser	0.30
Slide rule	*22.95*	Grocery	1.00
Cards	0.25	Grocery	9.14
Milk	0.98	R Digest	0.35
Postage	0.47	Notebook	0.75
Rent	25.00	Grocery	0.15
Paper	1.00	Car registration	2.50
R. Digest	0.35	Grocery	0.39
Milk	0.69	Scrubber	0.10
Postage	0.25	Anacin	0.25
Unaccounted	2.14		

Total $821.94

www.ingramcontent.com/pod-product-compliance
Lightning Source LLC
Chambersburg PA
CBHW030008290326

41934CB00005B/257